INTRODUCTION

STARTING WITH WRITING WILL BE EASY AND FUN FOR YOUR LITTLE ONE WITH THIS COLORFUL ARABIC READ AND WRITE WORKBOOK.
IN THIS WORKBOOK, YOU WILL FIND EXERCISES FOR PRACTICING ARABIC LETTERS FROM "ALIF" TO "YAA".
THE FIRST STEP TO LEARNING THE ARABIC LANGUAGE IS TO LEARN AND PRACTICE THE CHARACTERS,
THE WORKBOOK CONTAINS ILLUSTRATIONS TO HELP YOUR CHILD RECOGNIZE EACH LETTER IN BASIC VOCABULARY WORDS AND THE EXACT WAY TO PRONOUNCE.

AFTER FINISHING THIS WORKBOOK YOUR CHILD WILL BE ABLE TO:
1 WRITE THE PROPER SHAPE OF EACH LETTER.
2 LEARN HOW TO READ ARABIC LETTERS CORRECTLY.
3 LEARN SOME ARABIC WORDS.

THIS WORKBOOK IS RECOMMENDED FOR:
HOMESCHOOLING
PRESCHOOL
KINDERGARTEN
NURSERY

CONTENT

FIRST, LET'S FOLLOW THE
DOTTED LINES AND HELP
OUR FRIENDS

أولاً ، لنتبع الخطوط المنقطة
ونساعد أصدقاءنا

help the bees to find flowers and return home

ساعد النحل على إيجاد الزهور والعودة للمنزل -

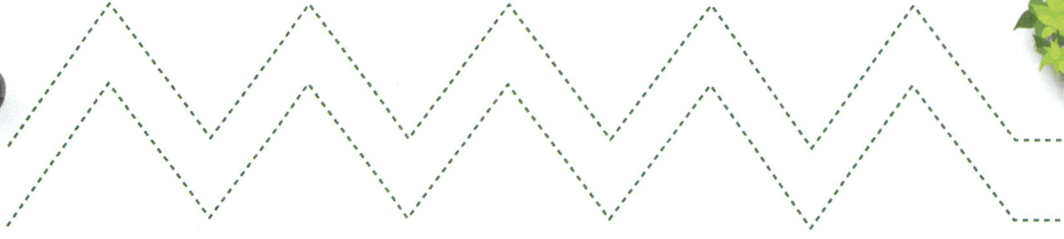

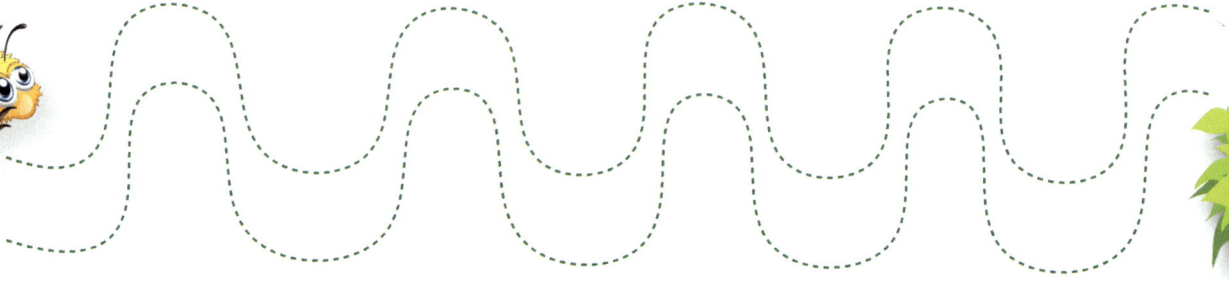

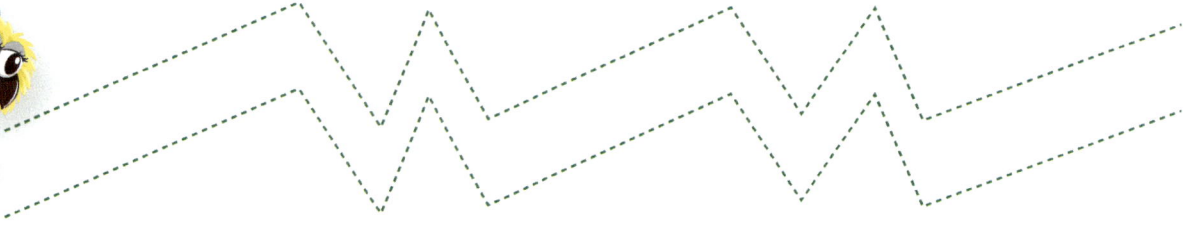

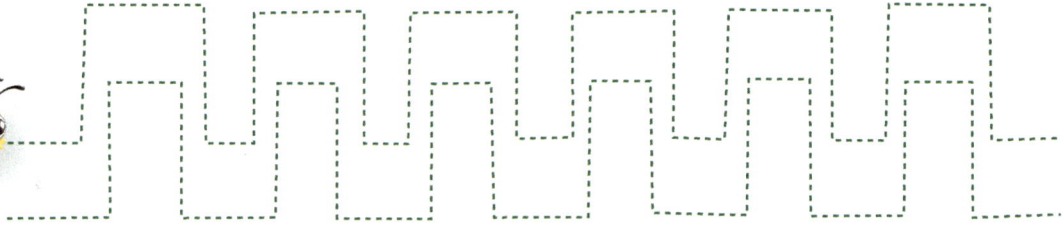

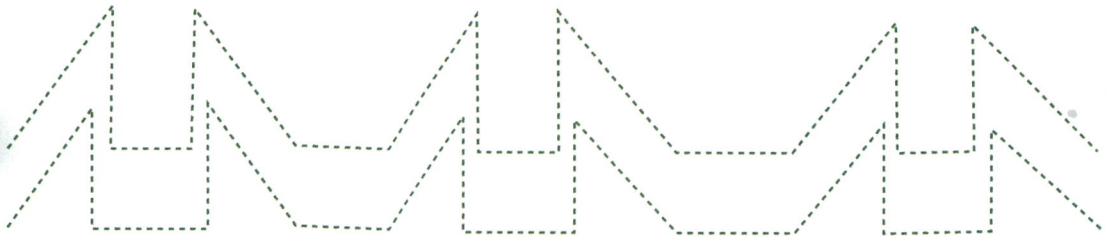

4

- help the dogs to return home

- ساعد الكلاب على العودة إلى ديارهم

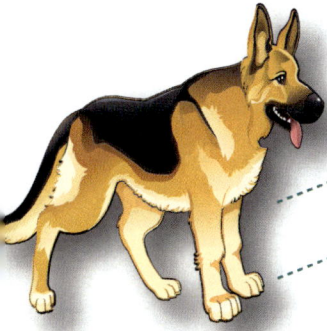

5

- help the little pirets to find treasure island

- ساعد القراصنة الصغار في العثور على جزيرة الكنز

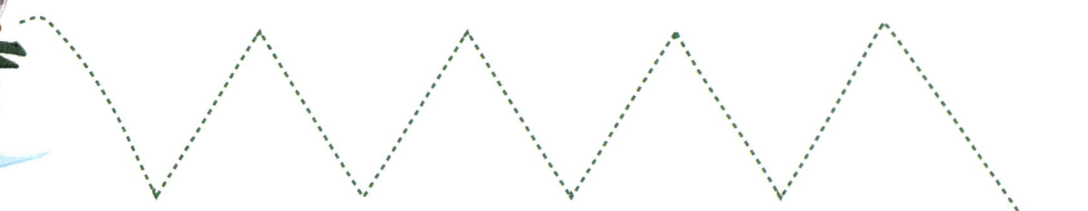

help the racing car to finish the race

- ساعد سيارة السباق على إنهاء السباق

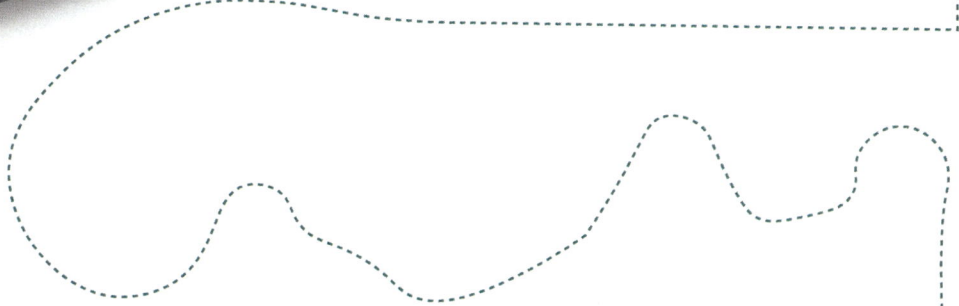

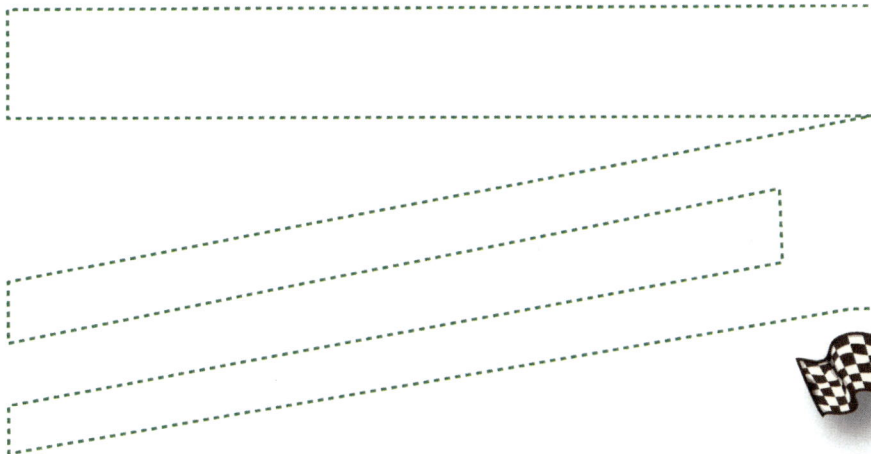

FINISH

1

2 1 3

LET'S NOW PRACTICE ARABIC ALPHABETS WRITING AND READING

لنبدأ الآن في كتابة وقراءة الأبجدية العربية

Alif makes the sound 'ai' as in air   اسد   Asad

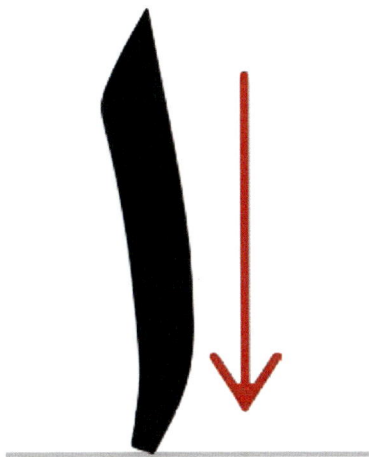

Read

Remember to start on this side in Arabic

Write

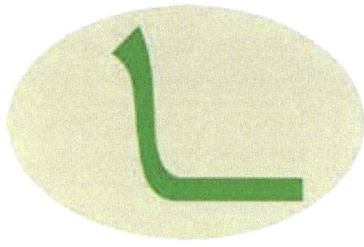

بَابٌ   أَرْنَبٌ

اا

ا ا ا ا

ب ب ب ب

اا با تا تا طا با را

سا حا طا عا طا فا

كا ية ها ها وا نا

Ba makes the sound 'ba' as in bat   بطّة   **Ba**tta

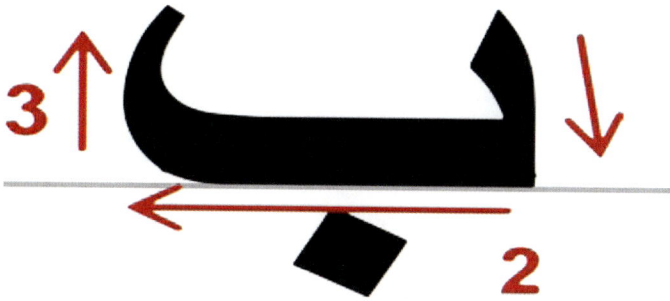

Read

ب ب ب ب ب ب ب ب ب

Write

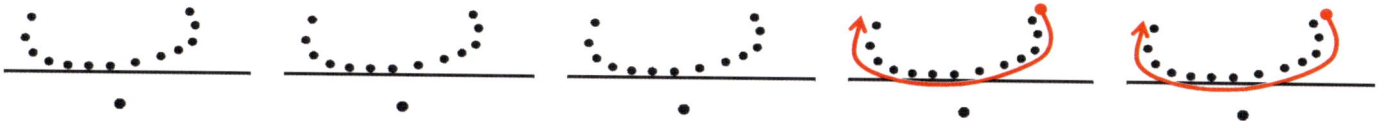

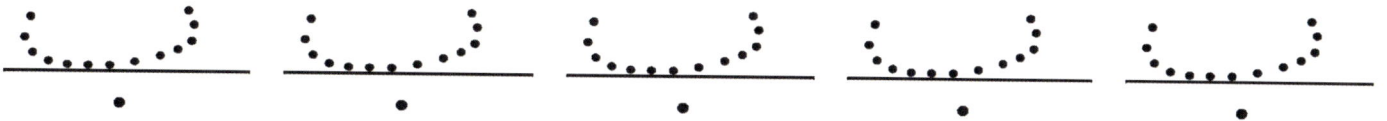

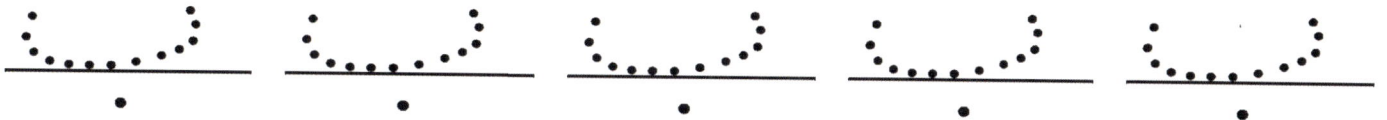

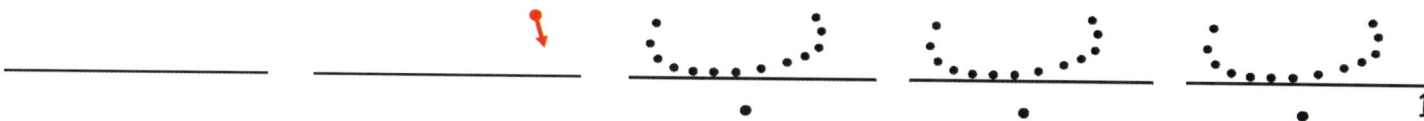

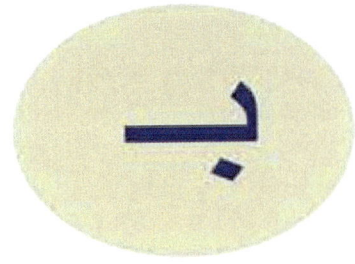

بـ بـ بـ ب

كَلْبٌ   سَبُّورَةٌ   بَقَرَةٌ

ب ـب ـبـ ببب

بـ بـ بـ

ـبـ ـبـ ـبـ

ـب ـب ـب

ببب ببب ببب

Ta makes the sound 'ta' as in Ta   Taaj تاج ج

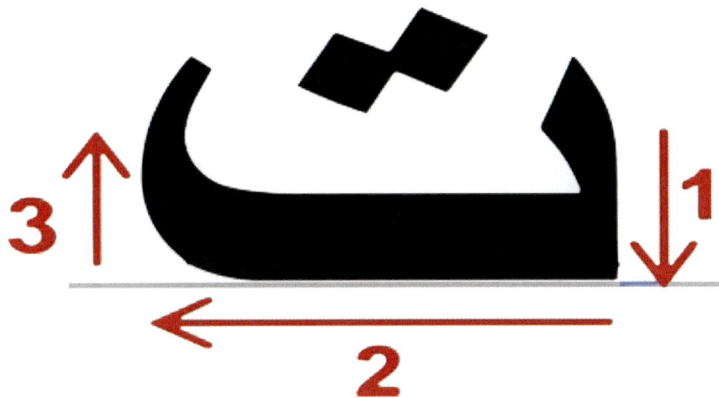

Read

ت ت ت ت ت ت ت ت ت ت

Write

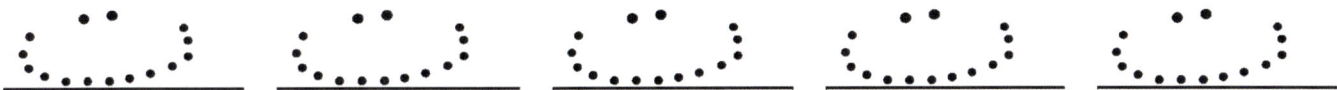

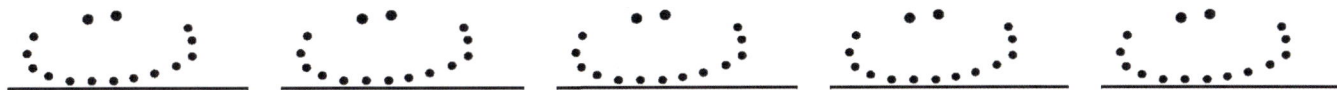

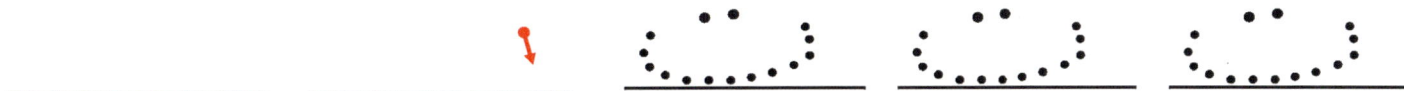

ت ت ت

بَيْتٌ   مَكْتَبٌ   تَنُّورَةٌ

ت تت ت ذ ت

ت   ت   ت

ت   ت   ت

ت   ت   ت

ت ت   ت ت

Tha makes the sound '**tha**' as in **tha**nk   Tha'lab ثَعلب

Read

Write

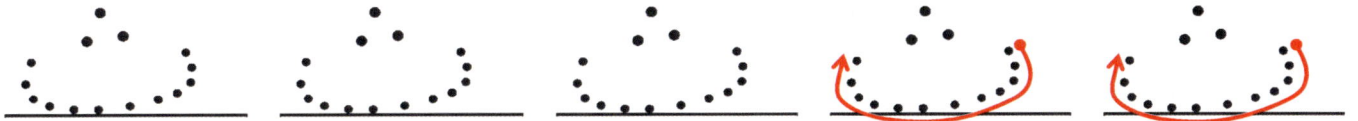

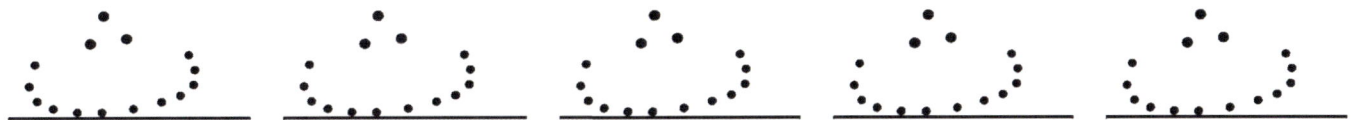

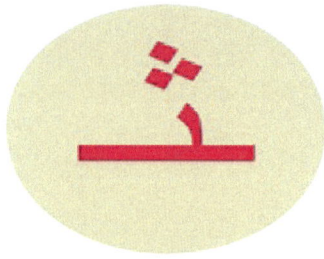

ثـ   ـثـ   ـث

مُثَلَّثٌ   كُمَّثْرَى   ثَعْلَبٌ

ث ث ث ث ث ث

ث   ث   ث

ـثـ   ـثـ   ـثـ

ـثـ   ـثـ   ـثـ

ـث   ـث   ـث

Jeem makes the sound 'ja' as in jam

Jamal مَلجَ

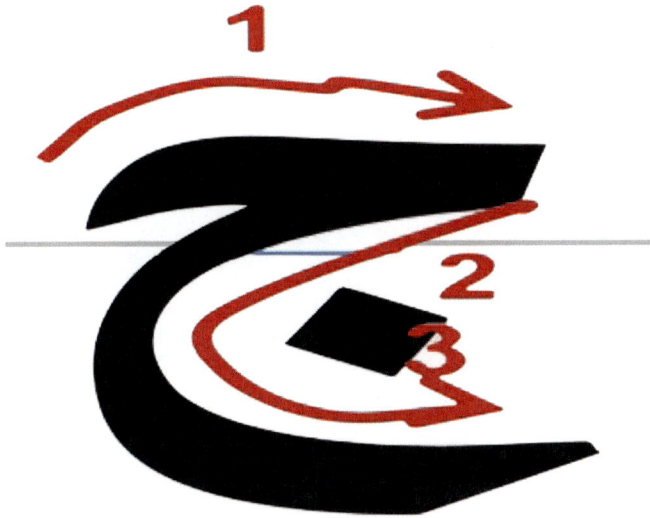

Jeem sits be-low the line

read

ج ج ج ج ج ج

Write

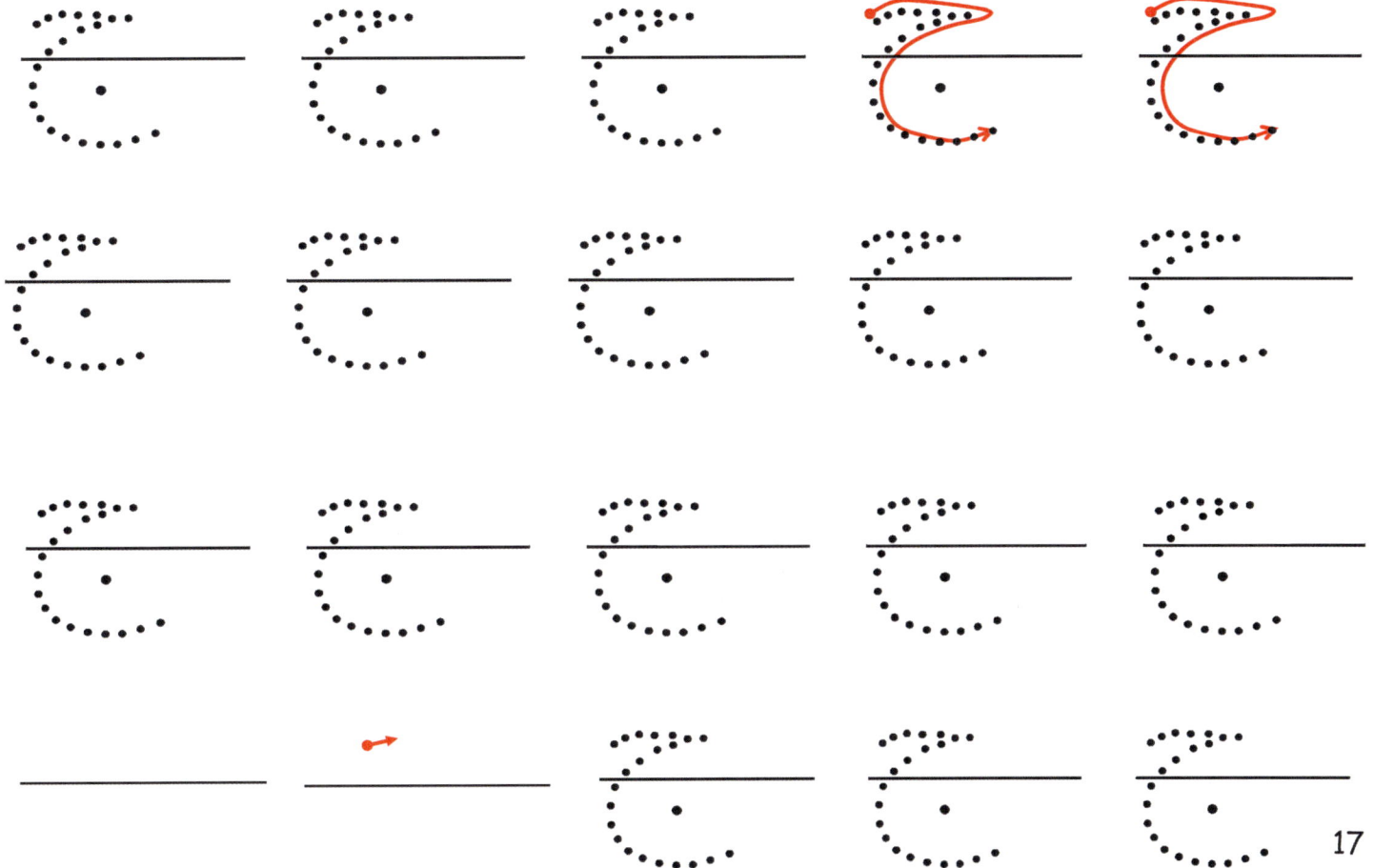

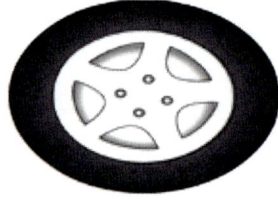

جـ جـ جـ

ثَلْجٌ   عَجَلَةٌ   جَيْبٌ

جـ جـ جـ ججج

Ha makes the sound '**ha**' as in **ha**ve

Harbaa **حرب**اء

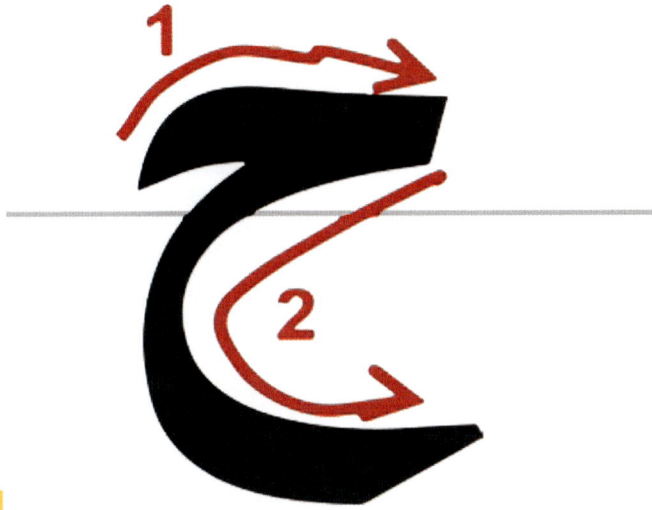

Read

Write

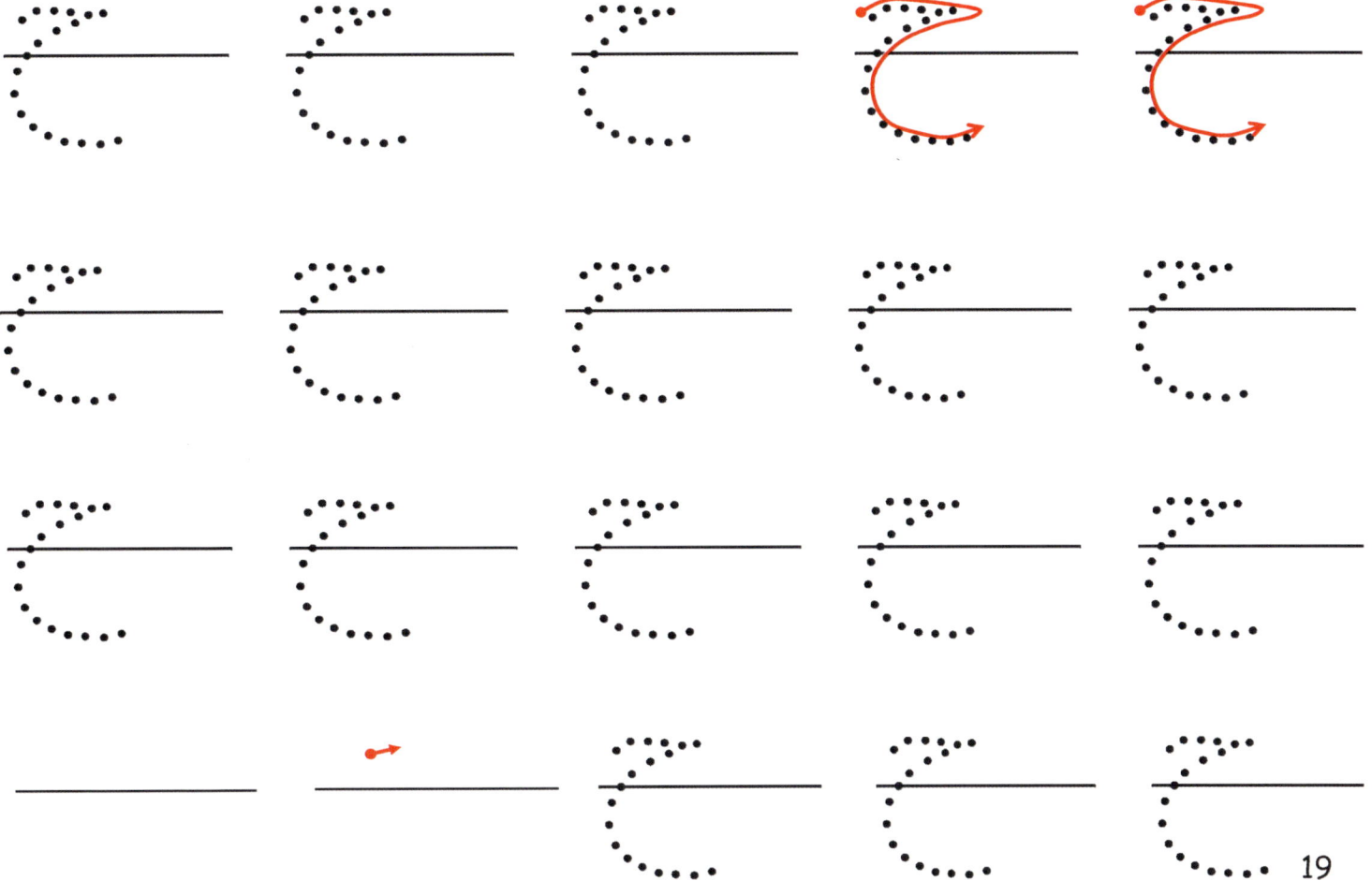

19

ح   ـد   ـح

مَسْبَحٌ   شَاحِنَةٌ   حَقِيبَةٌ

حح   حـ   ـد   ـد   حـ

Kha makes the sound 'kha' as in Khadija

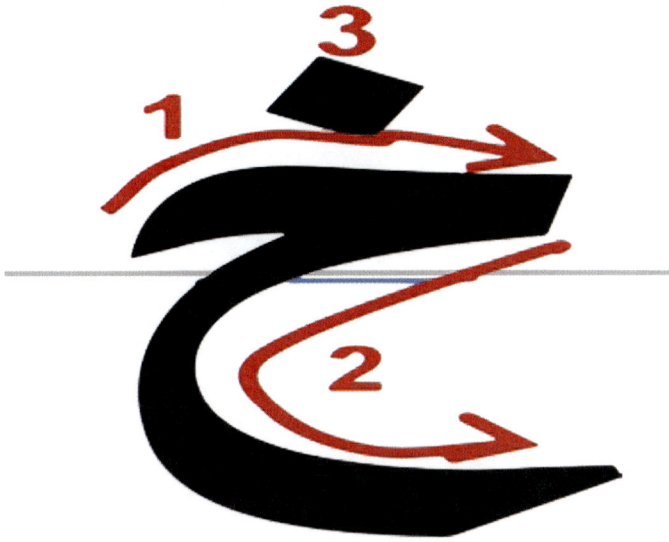

Read

Write

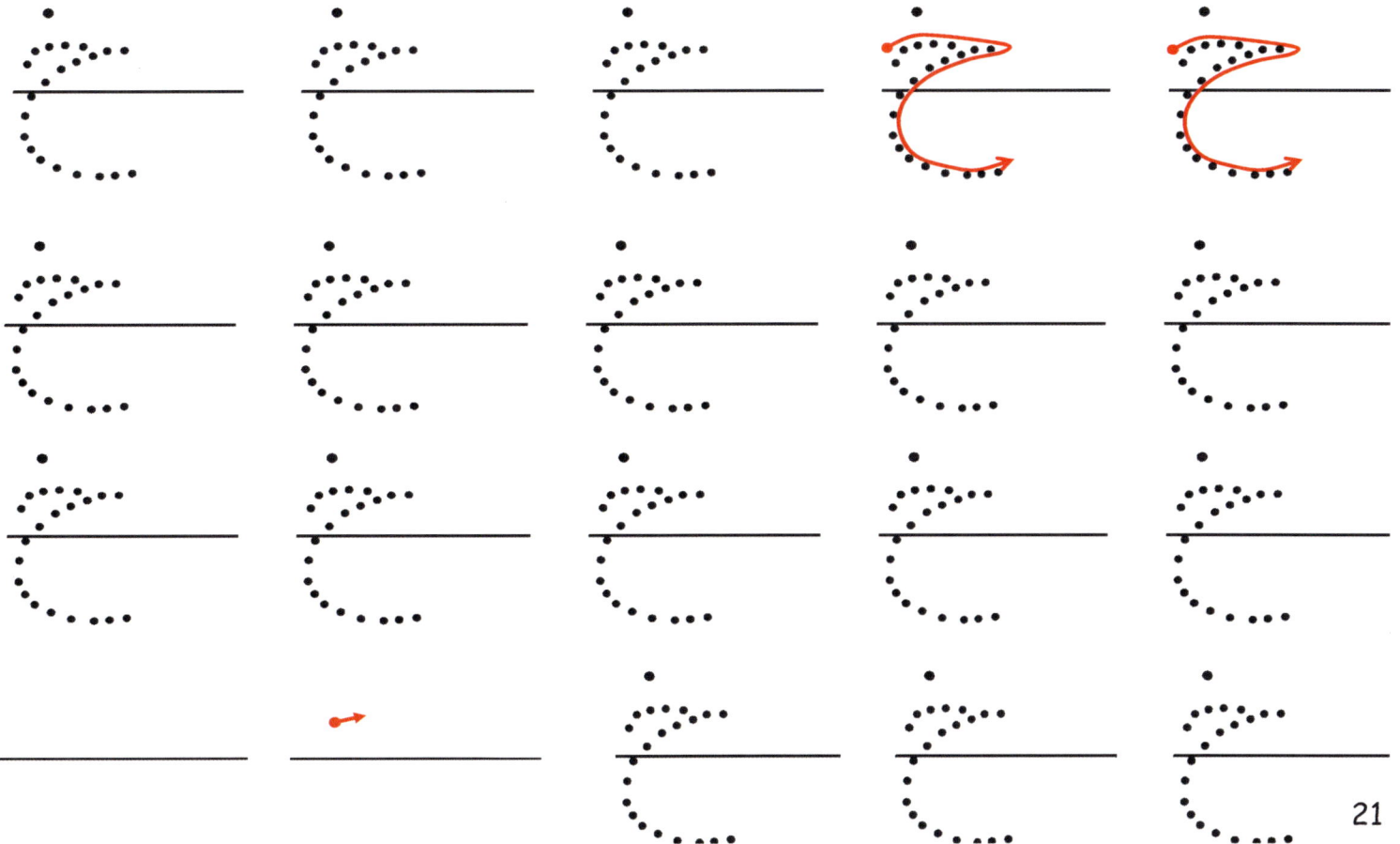

خ   خ   خ

بِطِّيخٌ   نَخْلَةٌ   خَرِيطَةٌ

خ خ خ خخخ

Dal makes the sound 'da' as in Dawood

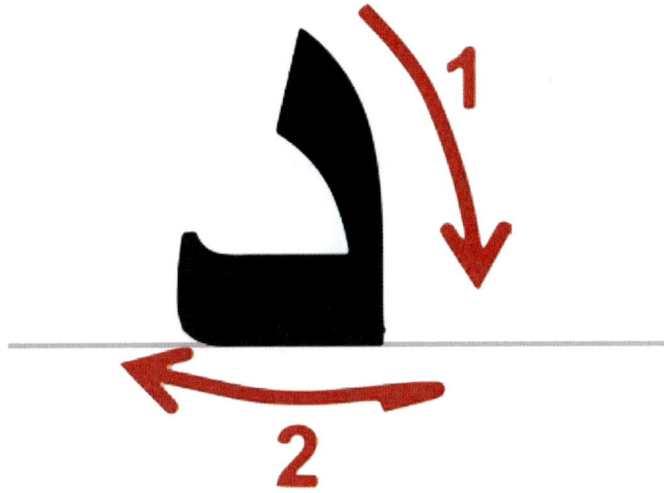

Read

ﺩ   ﺩ   ﺩ   ﺩ   ﺩ   ﺩ

Write

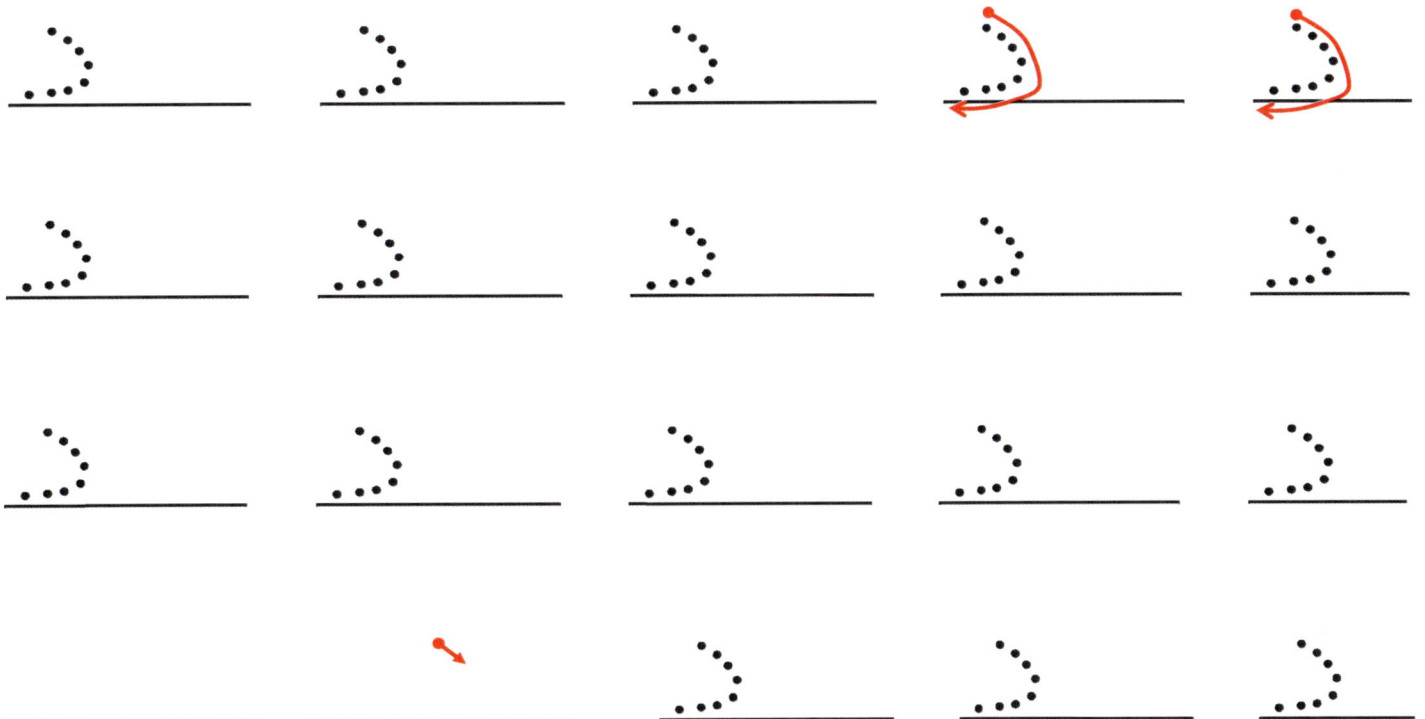

دـ د

مَقْعَدٌ دِيكٌ

دد

د   د   د   د

ـد   ـد   ـد   ـد

اد   بد   جد   دد   رد   سد

سد   طد   عد   فد   قد   كد

يد   ود   هد   مد   ند   لد

Dhal makes the sound 'tha' as in That

Dhahab ذهب

Read

Write

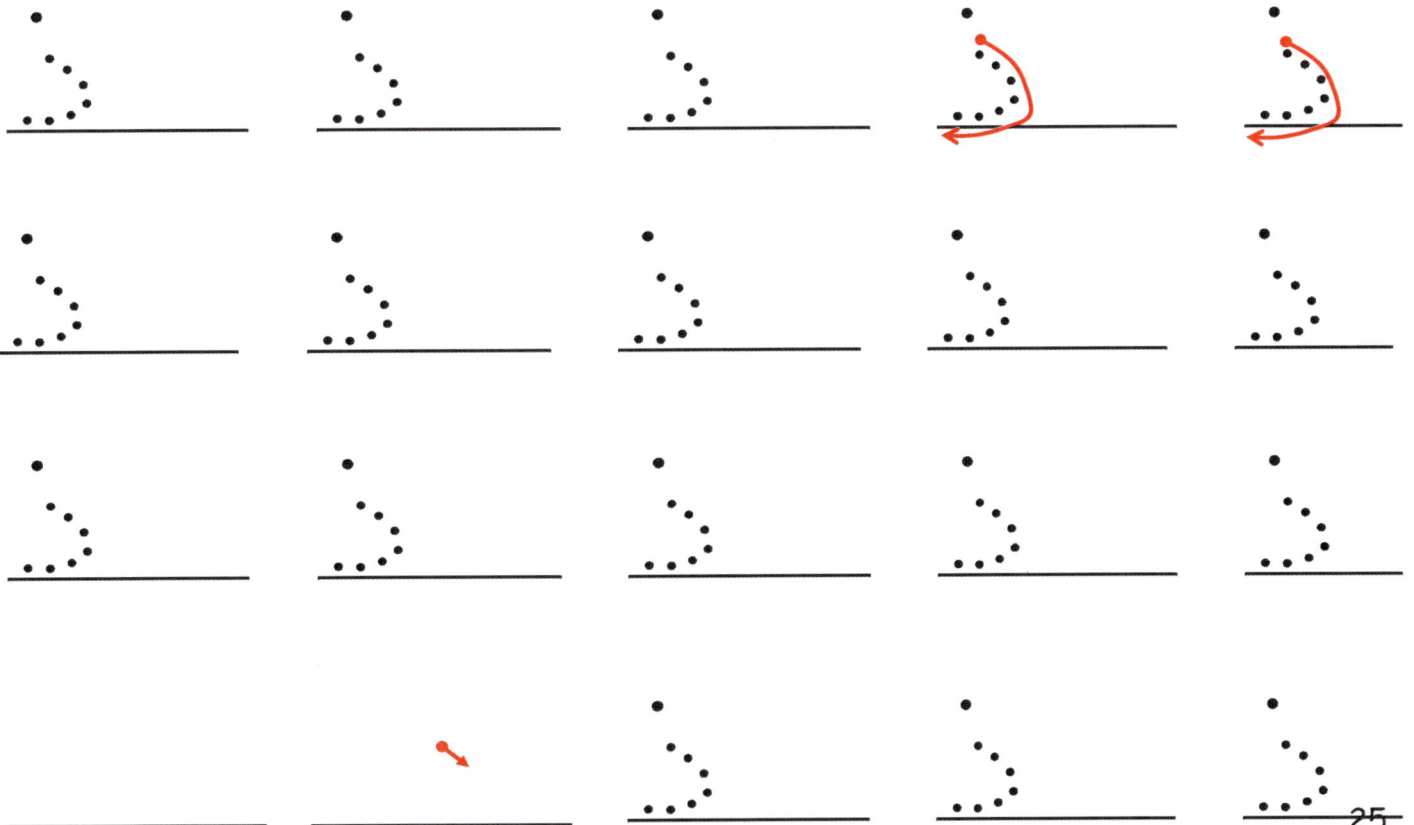

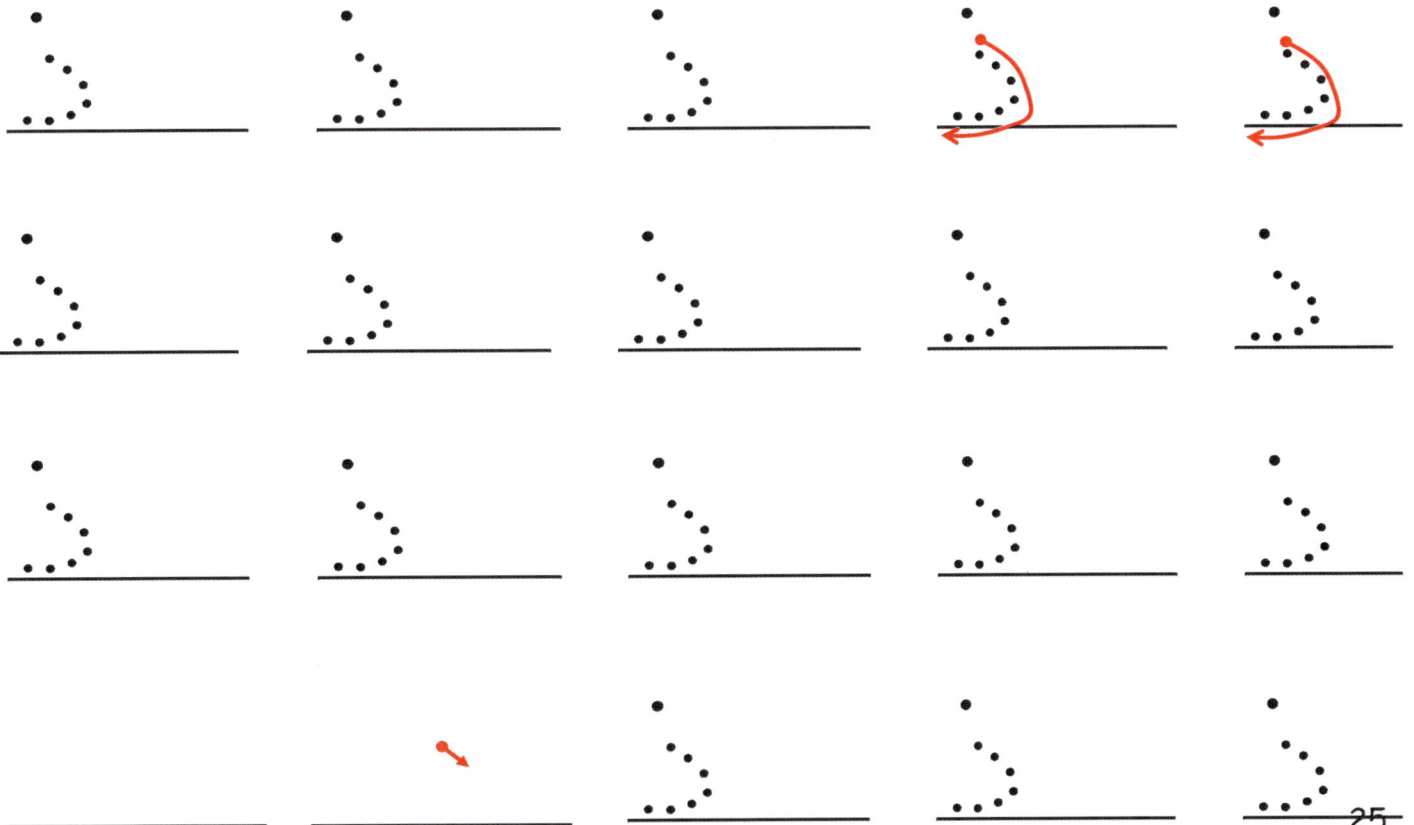

25

ذ ڎ

قُنْفُذٌ   ذُرَّةٌ

ذ ڎ

ذ ذ ذ

ذ ذ ذ

ذ ذ ذ ذ ذ ذ

ذ ذ ذ ذ ذ ذ

ذ ذ ذ ذ ذ ذ

Ra makes the sound 'ra' as in Rat

رسّام Rassaam

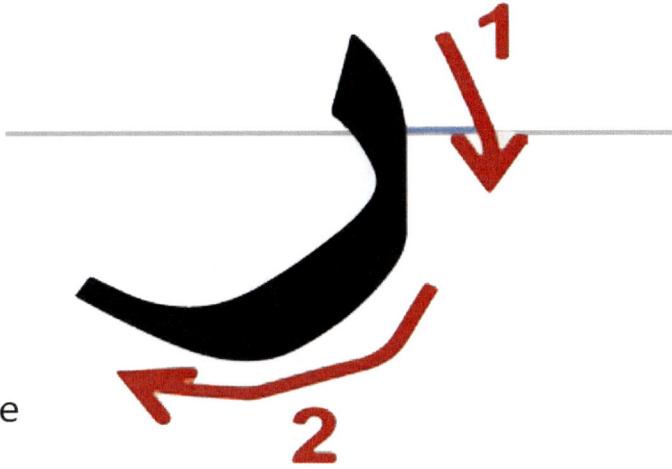

Ra sits
below
the line

Read

ر ر ر ر ر ر

Write

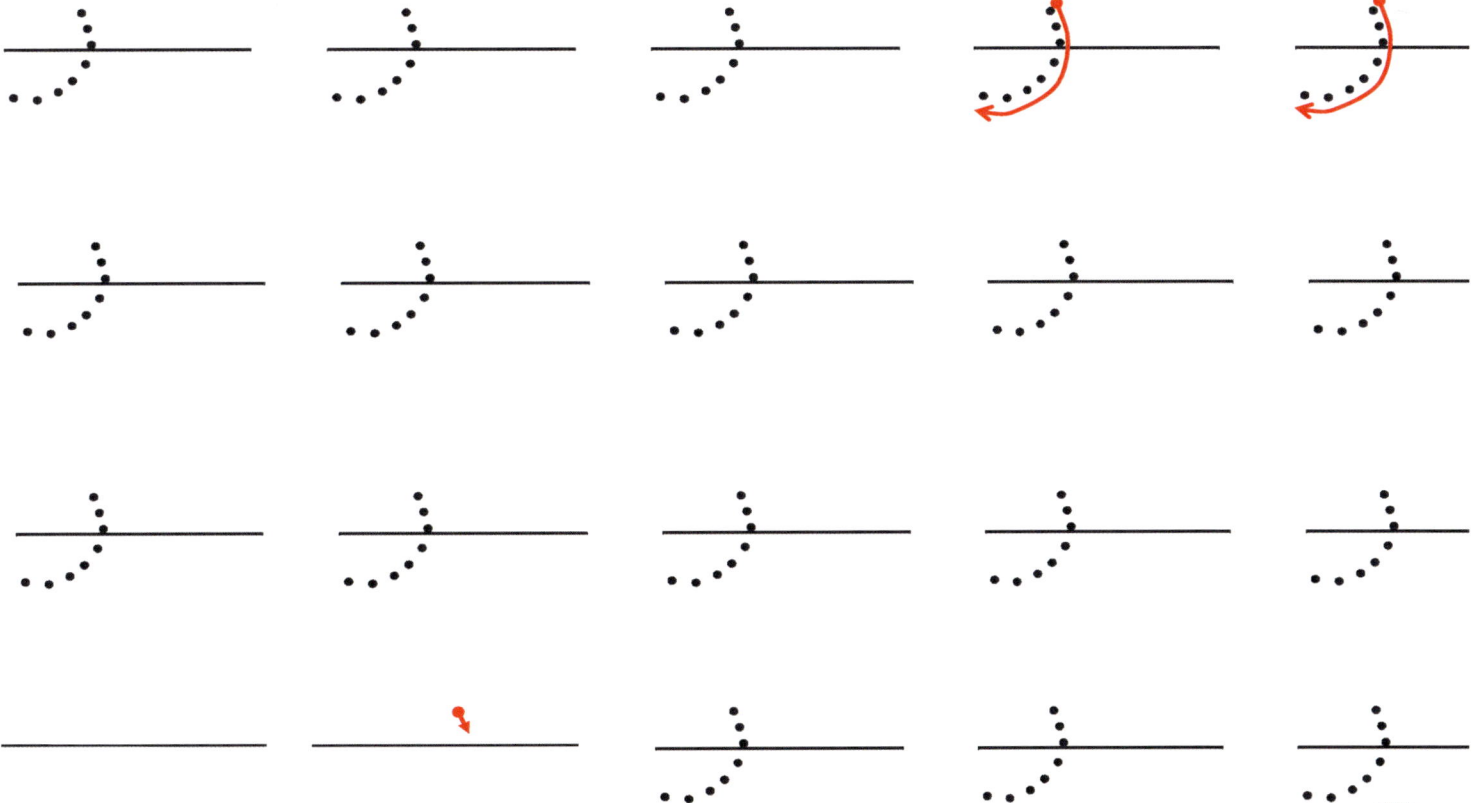

27

 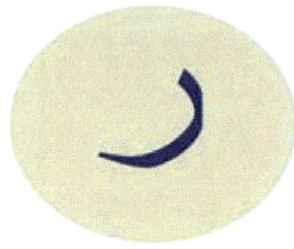

سَرِيرٌ   رِجْلٌ

ر ر

ﺮ ﺮ ﺮ

ﺮ ﺮ ﺮ ﺮ

ﺮ ﺮ ﺮ ﺮ ﺮ ﺮ

ﺮ ﺮ ﺮ ﺮ ﺮ ﺮ

ﺮ ﺮ ﺮ ﺮ ﺮ ﺮ

Za makes the sound 'za' as in Zakariya

Zahra زهرة

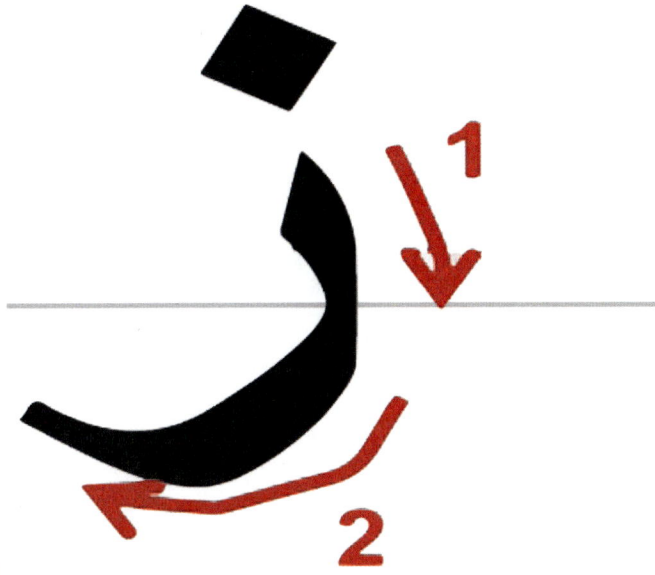

Read

ز ز ز ز ز ز

Write

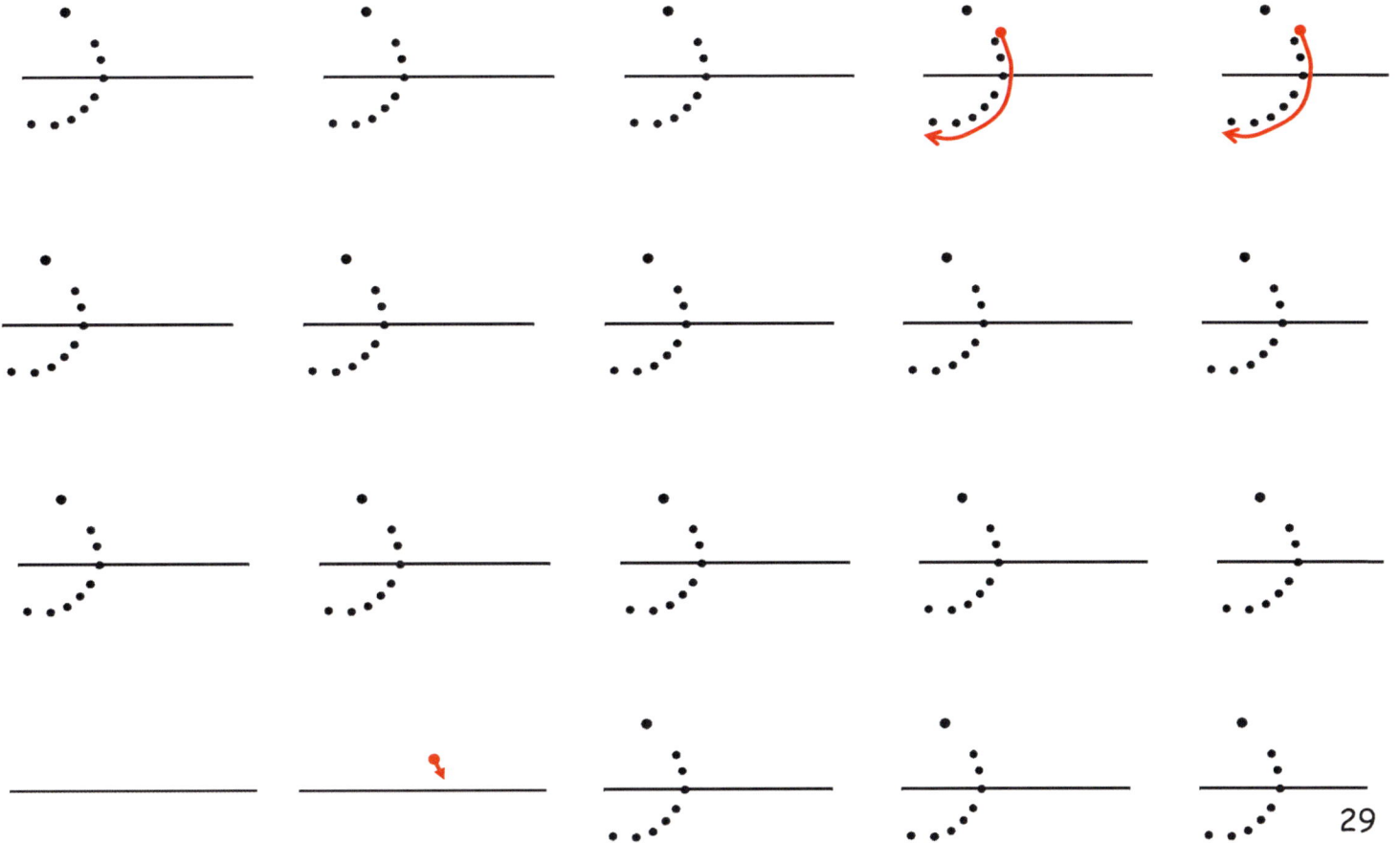

29

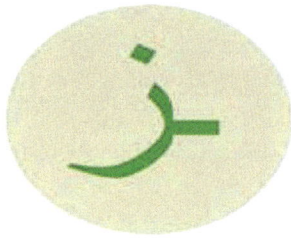

زـ   ز

خُبْزٌ   زَهْرَةٌ

ز ـز

ز ز ز

ـز ـز ـز

ز ز ز ز ز

ز ز ز ز ز

ز ز ز ز ز

Seen makes the sound 'sa' as in **sa**nd سمكة **Sa**maka

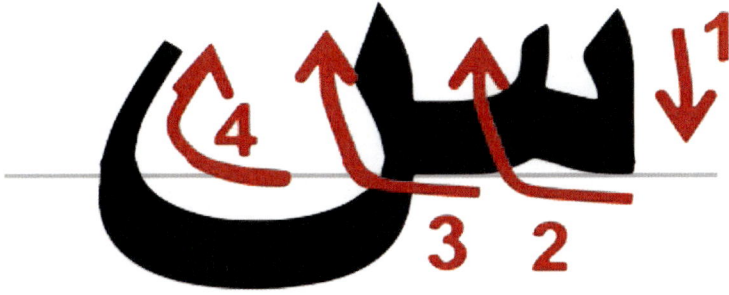

Read

س س س س س س

Write

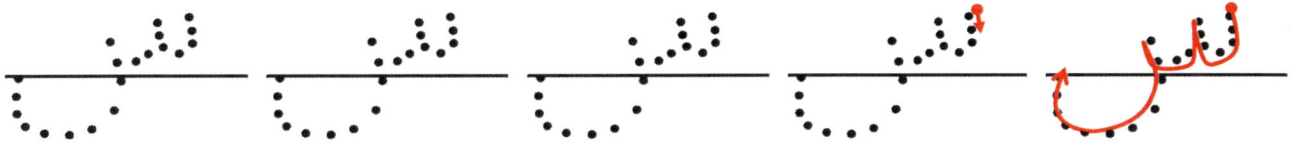

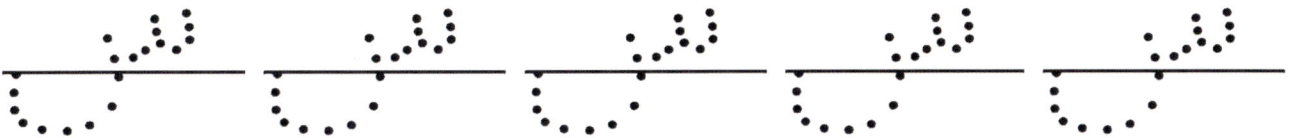

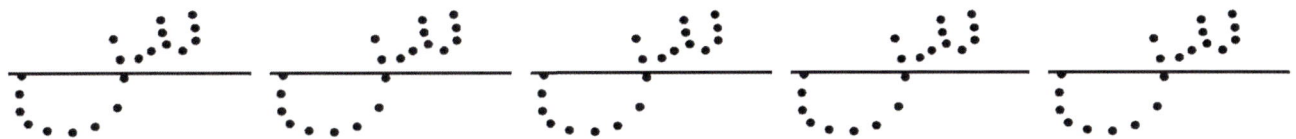

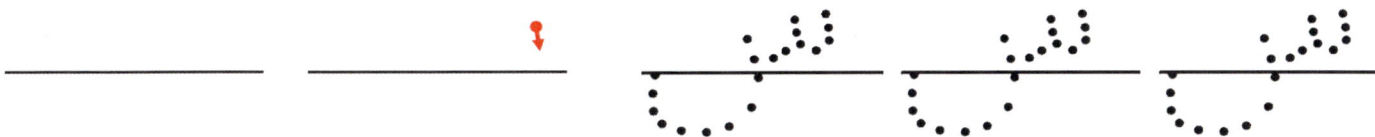

31

شَمْسٌ مِسْطَرَةٌ سَفِينَةٌ

سـ ـسـ ـس سسس

sha**ms**   شـمس

Sheen makes the sound 'sha' as in **sha**rk

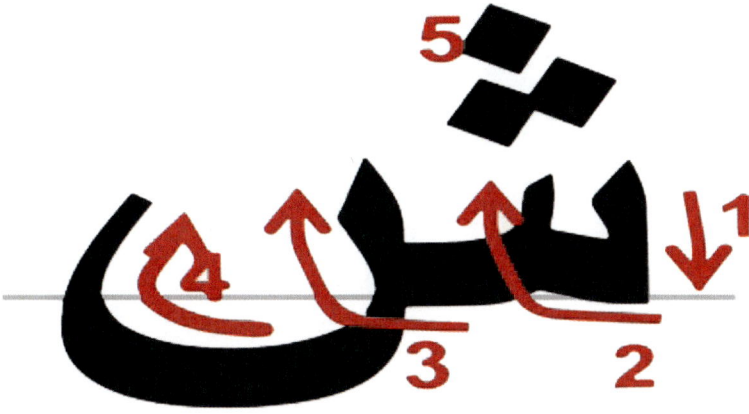

Read

ش   ش   ش   ش   ش

Write

ش   ش   ش

مِشْمِشْ   عُشْبَةٌ   شَجَرَةٌ

شـ شـ ش ششش

صابون Saaboon

Saad makes the sound 'swa' as in sword

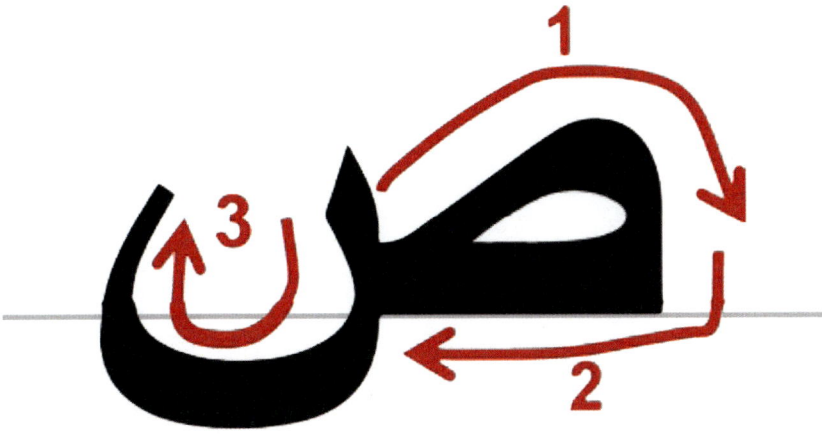

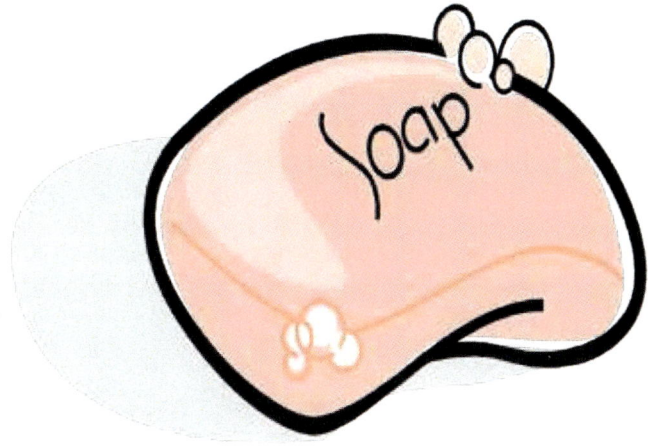

Read

ص ص ص ص ص

Write

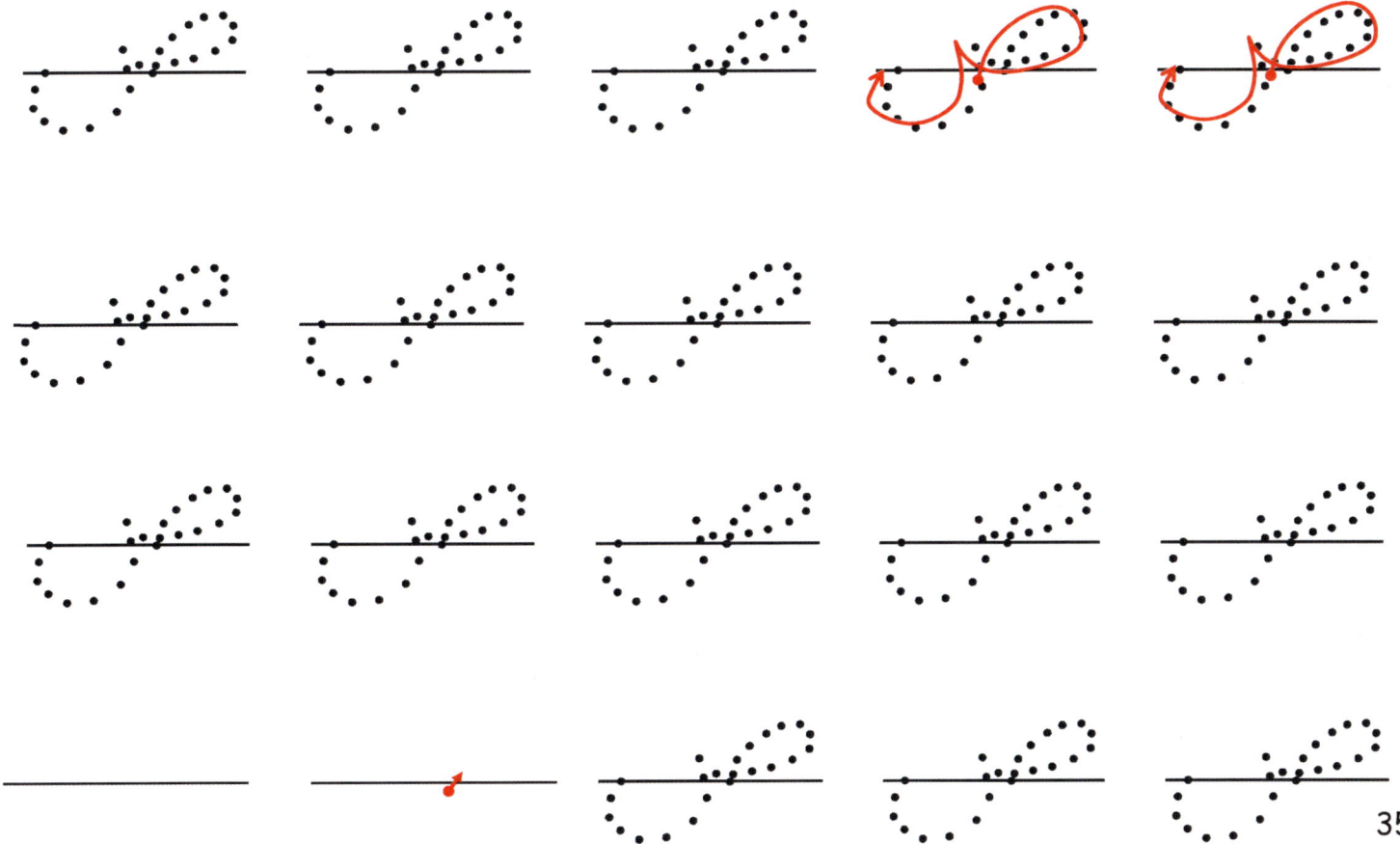

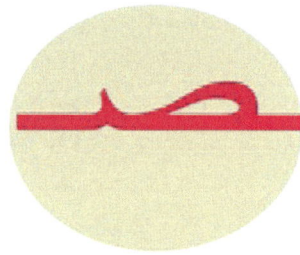

صـ صـ ـصـ ـص

مِقَصٌّ   مِصْبَاحٌ   صُنْدُوقٌ

صـ صـ ص صصص

Dafda'   ضفدع

Dhaad makes the sound '**dha**' as in **thou**

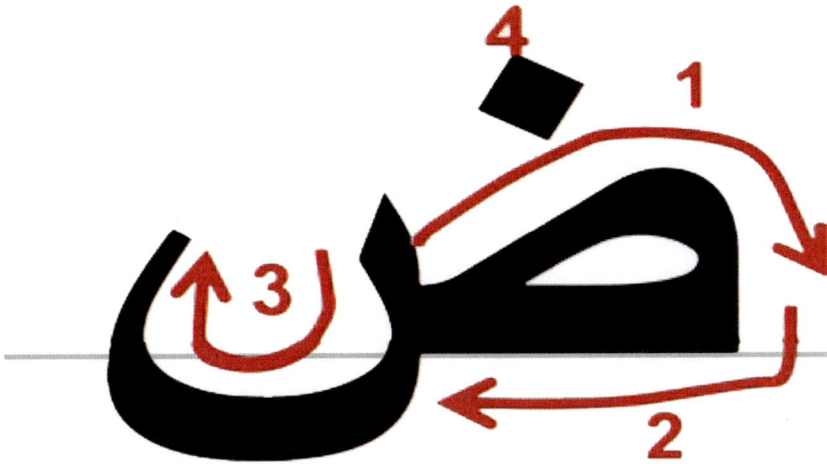

Read

ض ض ض ض

Write

ضَ   ضِ   ضُ

بَيْضٌ   مِنْضَدَةٌ   ضِرْسٌ

ضض ض ضض ض

ضـ   ضـ   ضـ

ـضـ   ـضـ   ـضـ

ـض   ـض   ـض

ـضـضـ   ـضـضـ   ـضـضـ

Ta makes the sound 'Ta'

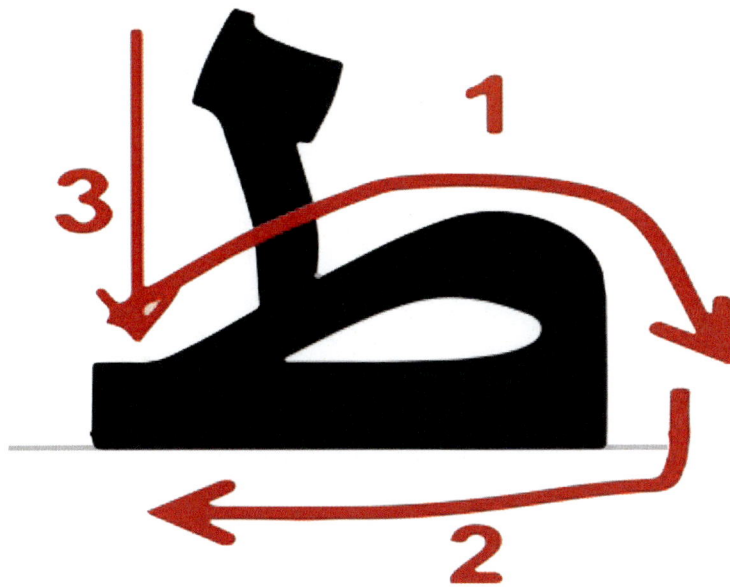

طاووس Tawoos

Read

Write

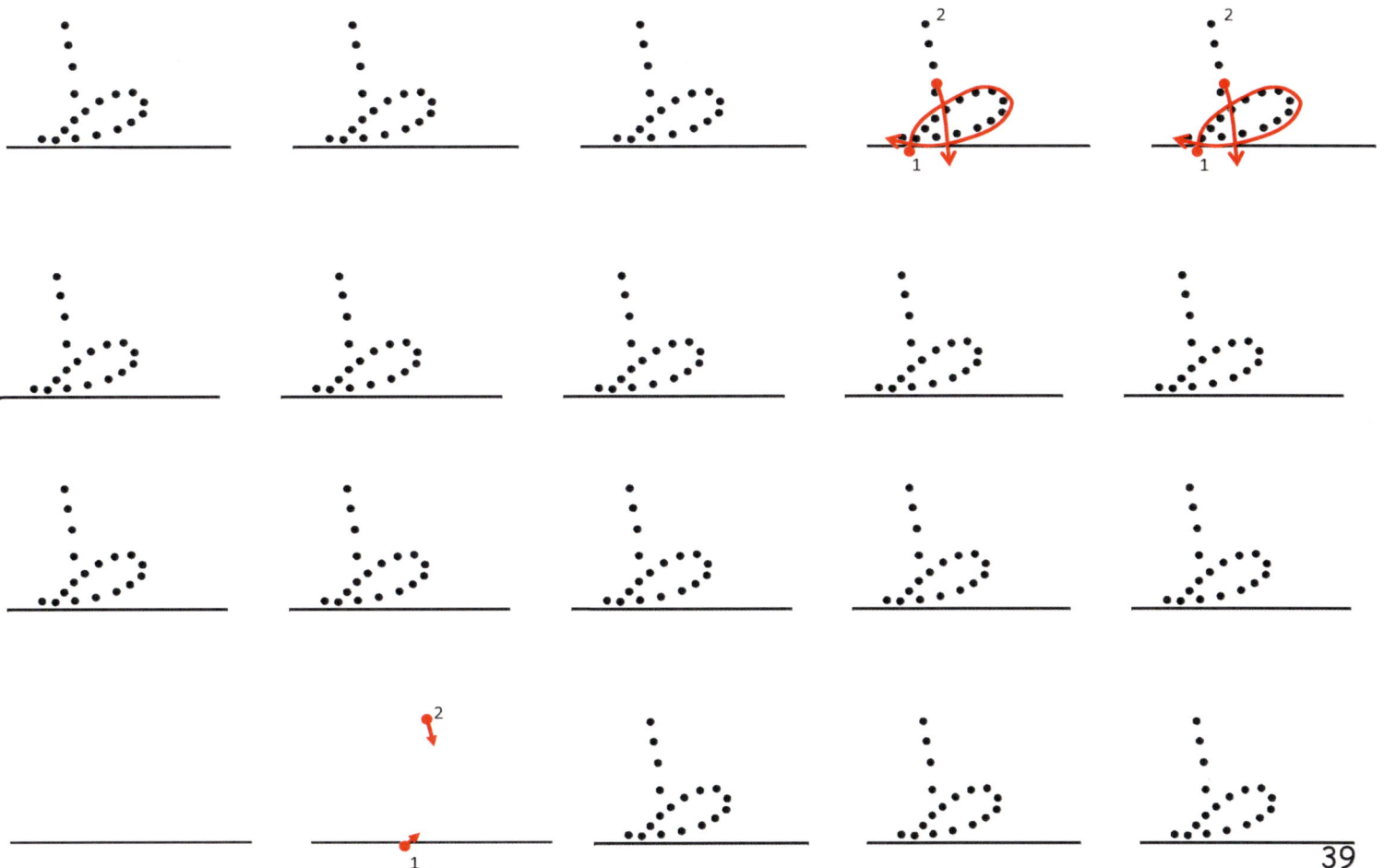

ط ط ط

مُشْطٌ   قِطَارٌ   طَيْرٌ

ط ططط ط ط ط ط

ط ط ط

ط ط ط

ط ط ط

ططط ططط

Dha makes the sound 'Dha'

 ظبي Dhabi

Read

Write

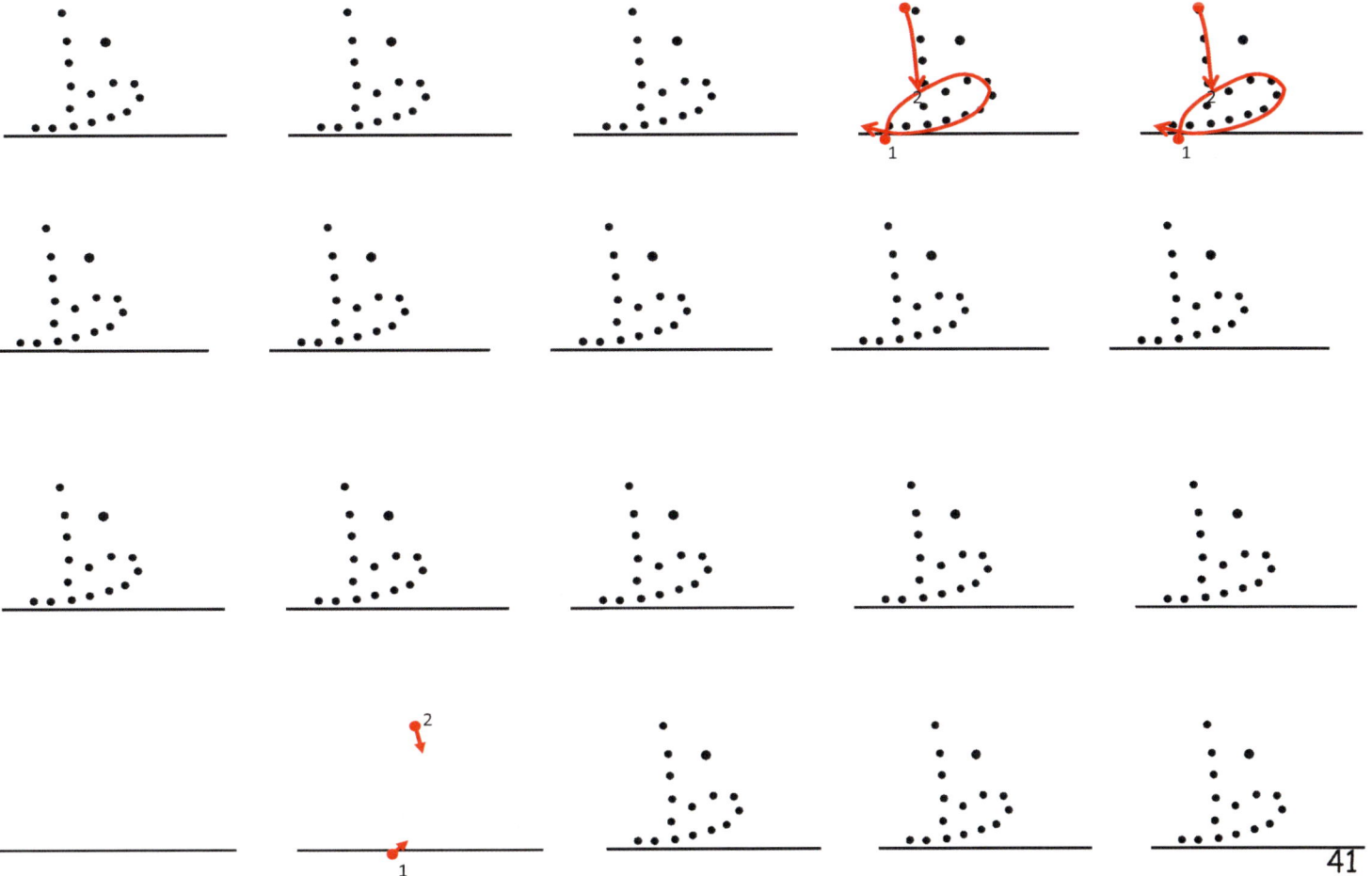

41

  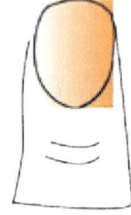

فَظٌّ   مِظَلَّةٌ   ظُفْرٌ

ظ ظ ظ ظظظ

ظ ظ ظ

ظ ظ ظ

ظ ظ ظ

ظظظ ظظظ

Ain makes the sound ''a' as in Abdullah

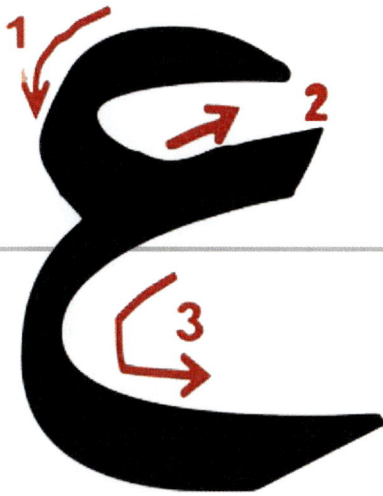

Read

Write

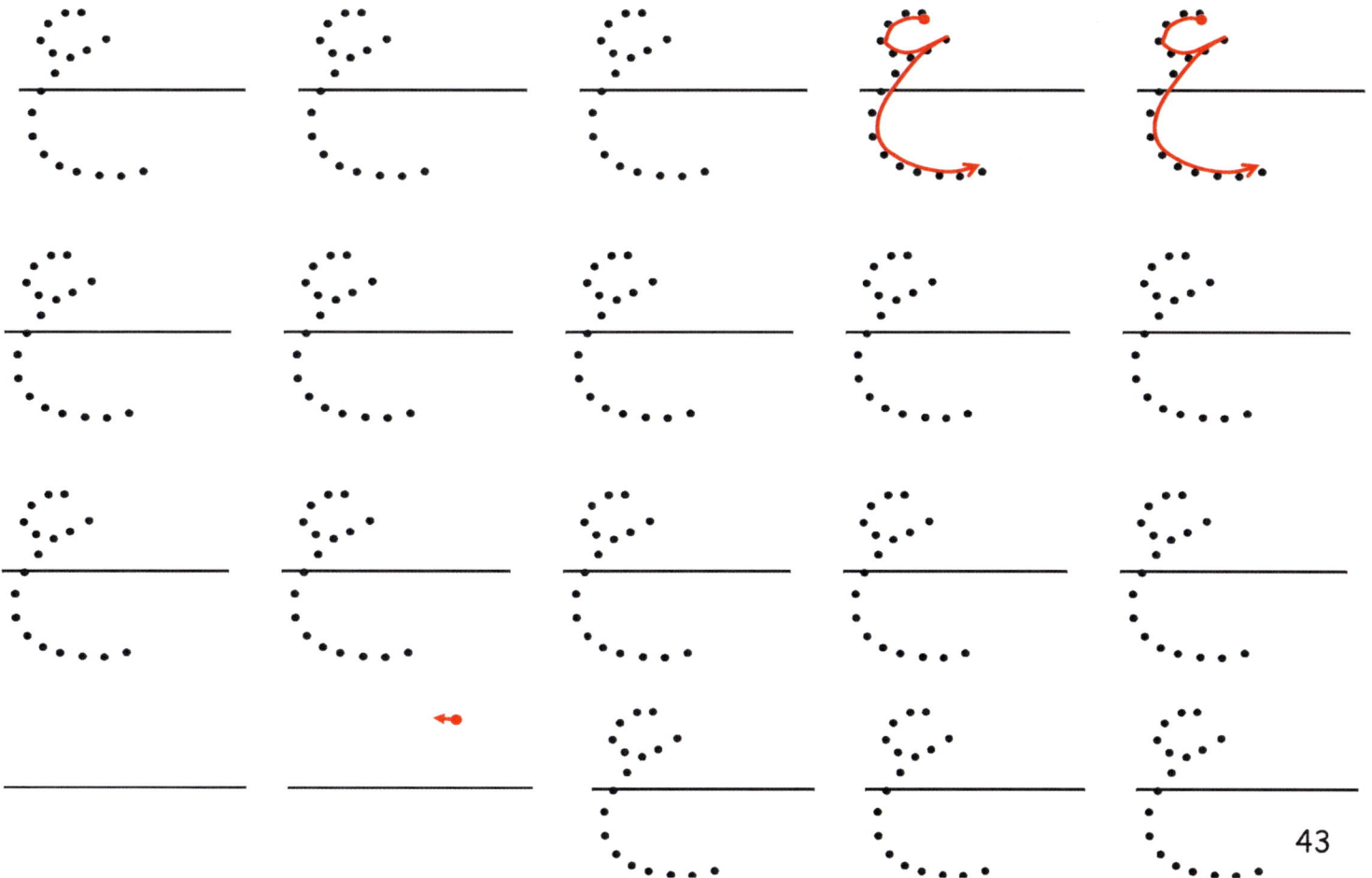

43

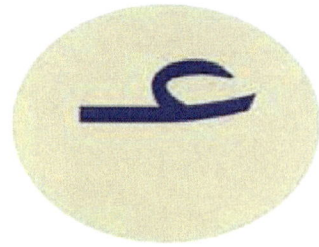

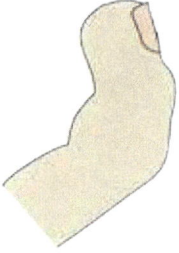

عـ	ـعـ	ع

إصْبَعٌ   مِعْطَفٌ   عِنَبٌ

عـ ـعـ ع عع

عـ .... عـ .... عـ ....

ـعـ .... ـعـ .... ـعـ ....

ع .... ع .... ع ....

ـعع .... ـعع ....

Gain makes the sound 'gha' as in Maghrib

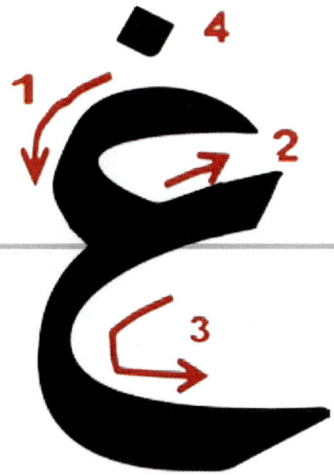

غسالة Gassaalah

Read

غ   غ   غ   غ   غ   غ

Write

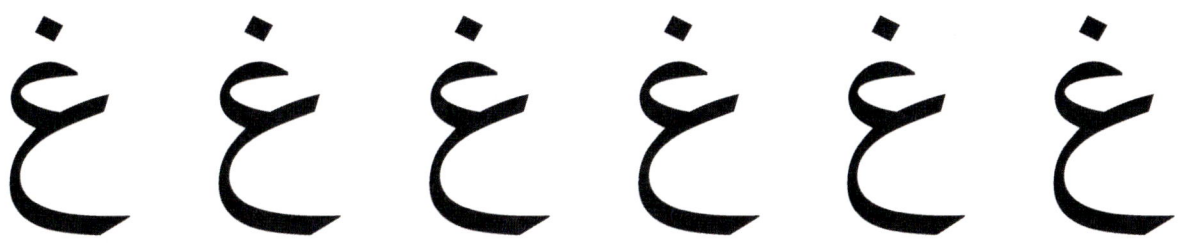

45

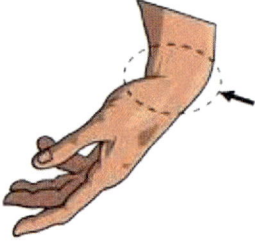

غـ ـغـ ـغ

غَيْمٌ | بَبْغَاءُ | رُسْغٌ

غ ـغ ـغـ غغغ

Fa makes the sound 'fa' as in fat   فَم   Fam

Read

ف   ف   ف   ف   ف   ف

Write

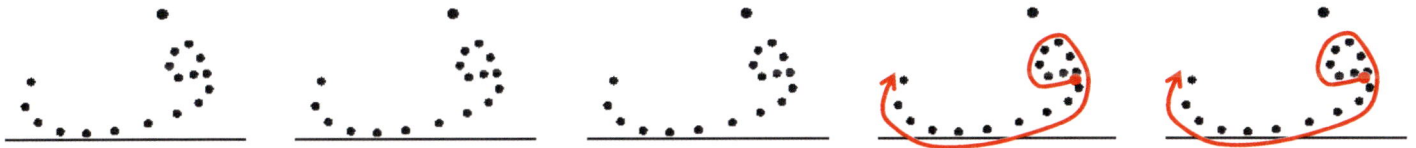

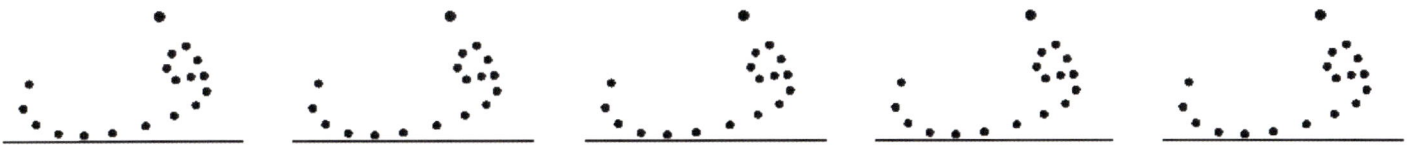

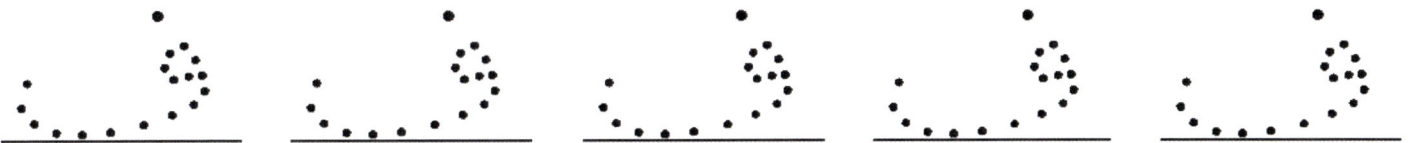

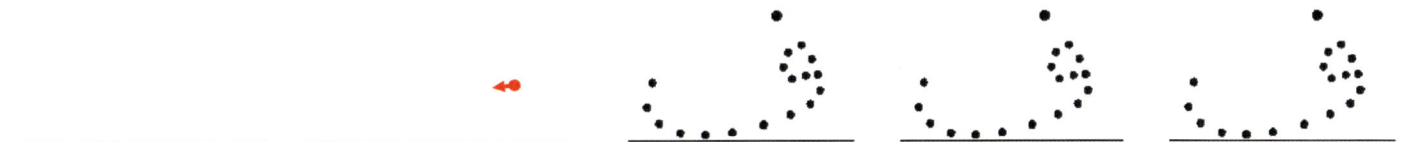

ف   ف   ف

أَنْفٌ   فِيلٌ   مِفْتَاحٌ   فِيلٌ

ف ف ف ففف

ف ....ف.... ....ف

....ف.... ....ف.... ....ف

....ف.... ....ف.... ....ف

....ففف.. ....ففف.. ....ففف..

Qaf makes the sound '**qa**'

Qamar قمر

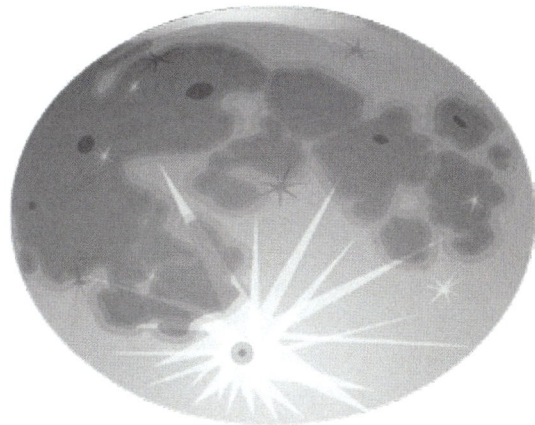

Read

ق ق ق ق ق

Write

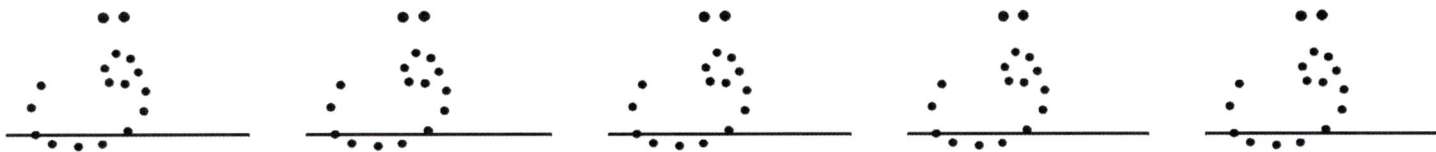

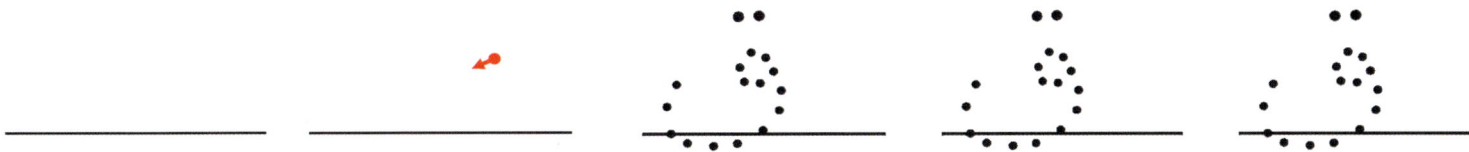

مِلْعَقَةٌ   طَرِيقٌ   قَلَمٌ

قـ ق ققق

ﻗـ ﻗـ ﻗـ

ﻗـ ﻗـ ﻗـ

ـﻖ ـﻖ ـﻖ

ﻗﻖ ﻗﻖ ﻗﻖ

Kaf makes the sound 'ka' as in ka'ba

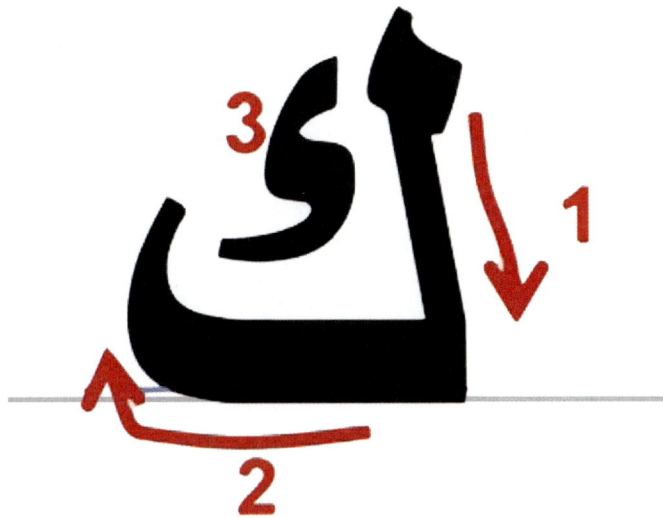

كعبة Ka'ba

Read

ك ك ك ك ك ك ك ك ك ك ك ك

Write

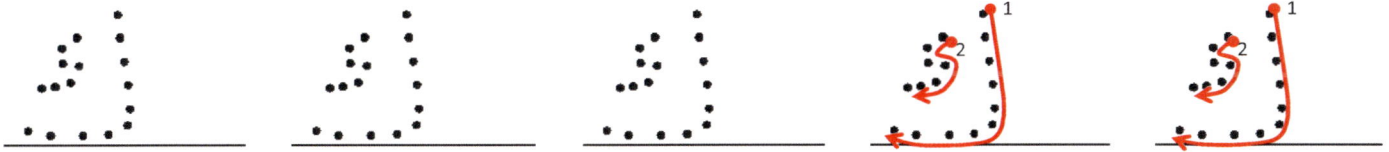

51

سَمَكٌ   مِكْوَاةٌ   كِتَابٌ

ك ك ك ككك

Laam makes the sound 'la' as in laugh لوز Lawz

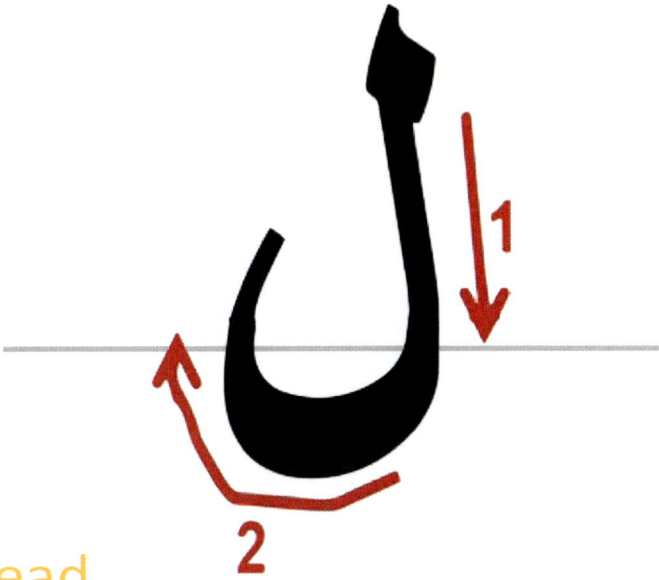

Read

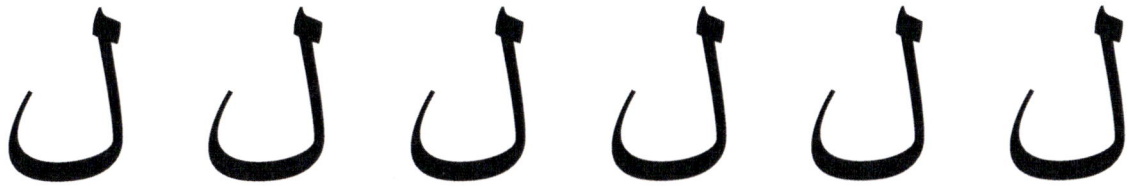

Write

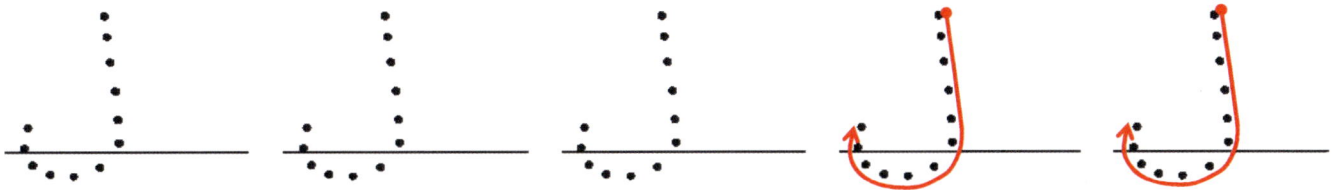

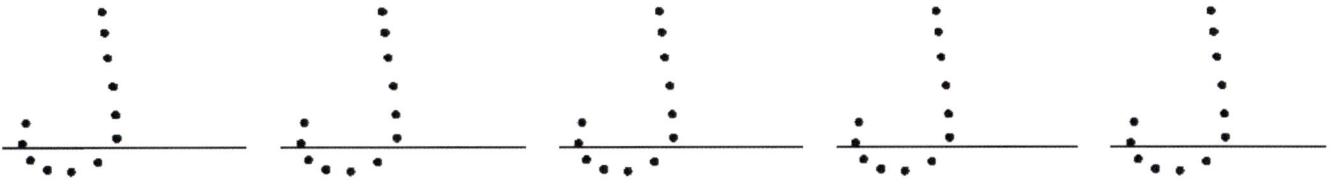

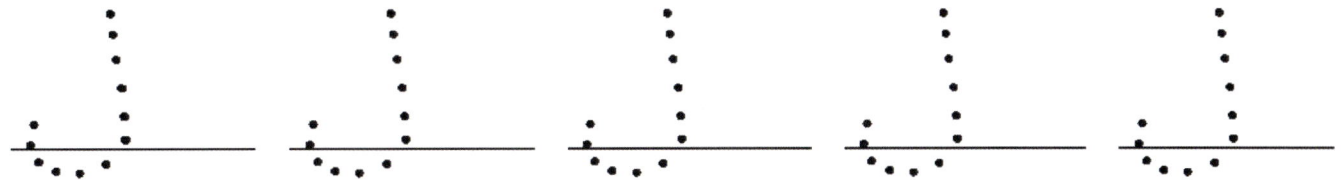

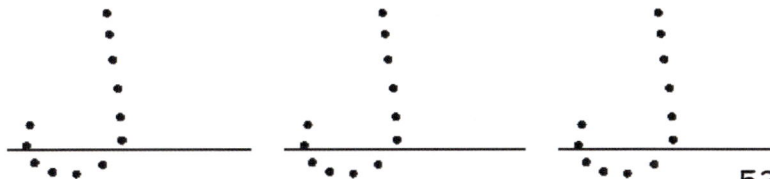

53

ل   لـ   ـل

بَصَلٌ   حَافِلَةٌ   لَحْمٌ

لـ لـ ل لل

ـ ـ ـ ـ

ـ ـ ـ ـ

ـل ـل ـل

لل لل لل

Masjid مسجد

Meem makes the sound 'ma' as in mark

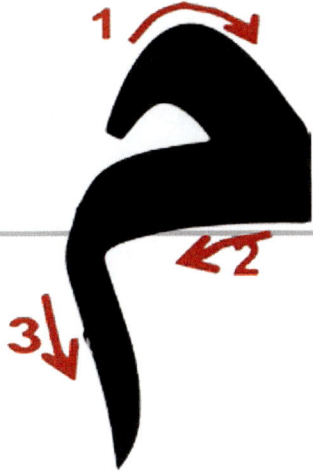

Read

م م م م م م

Write

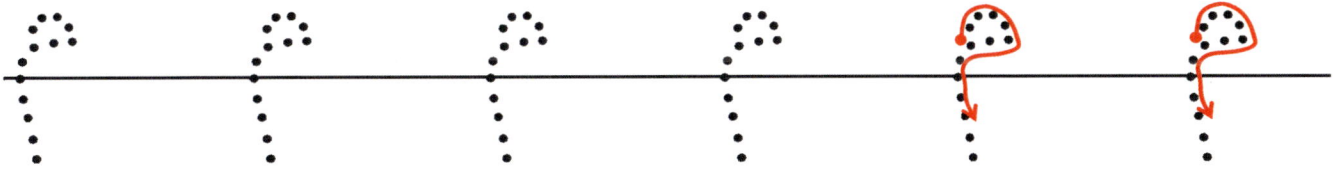

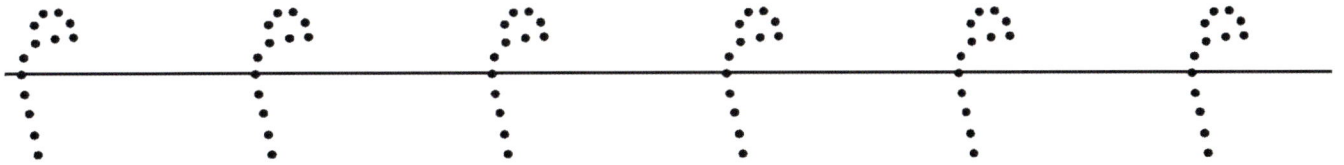

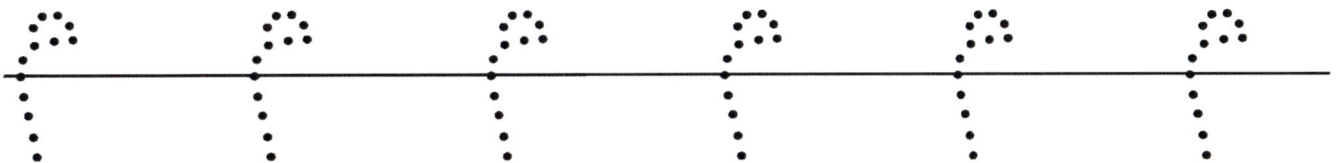

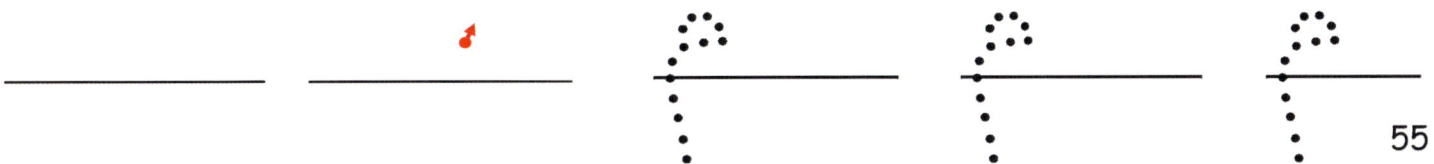

55

عَلَمٌ   نَمْلَةٌ   مِرْسَمٌ

ممم   ـم   ـمـ   مـ

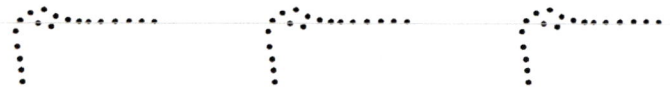

Noon makes the sound 'na' as in **Na**nny

نجم   **Na**jm

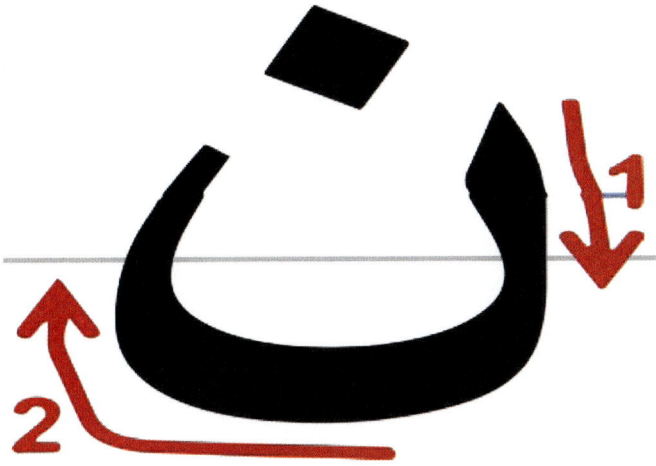

Read

ن ن ن ن ن ن ن

Write

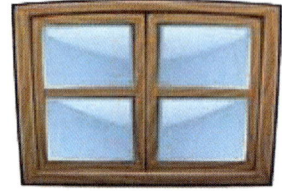

نْ	ـنْ	نـ

جُبْنٌ	فِنْجَانٌ	نَافِذَةٌ

ذ ـنْ نن

نـ ـنـ ـن

ـنـ ـنـ ـن

ـن ـنـ نـ

نن نن

Ha makes the sound 'ha' as in hat

هدية **Ha**diyah

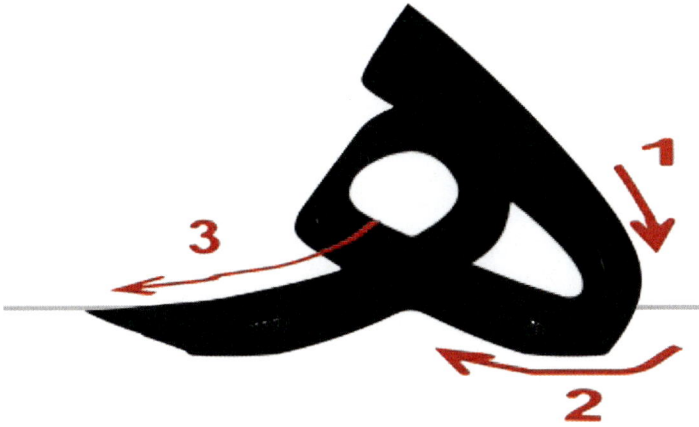

Read

Write

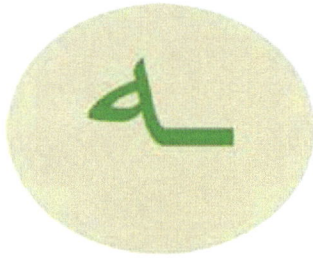  

وَجْهٌ   نَهْرٌ   هَاتِفٌ

هـ ـهـ ـه ههه

Waw makes the sound 'wo' as in wonder ورد Word

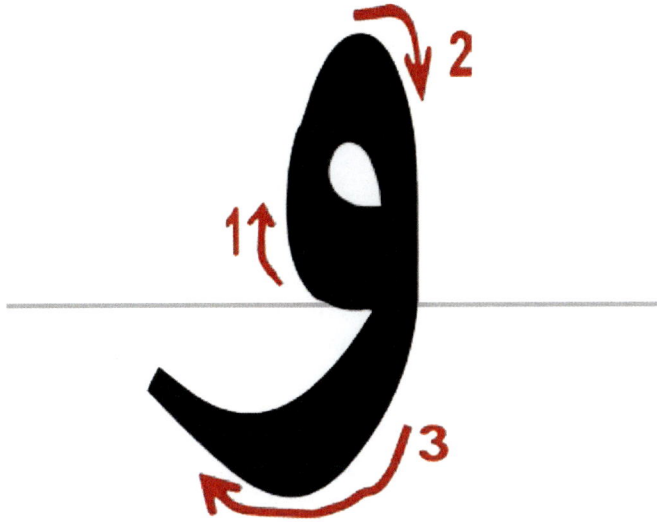

Read

و   و   و   و   و

Write

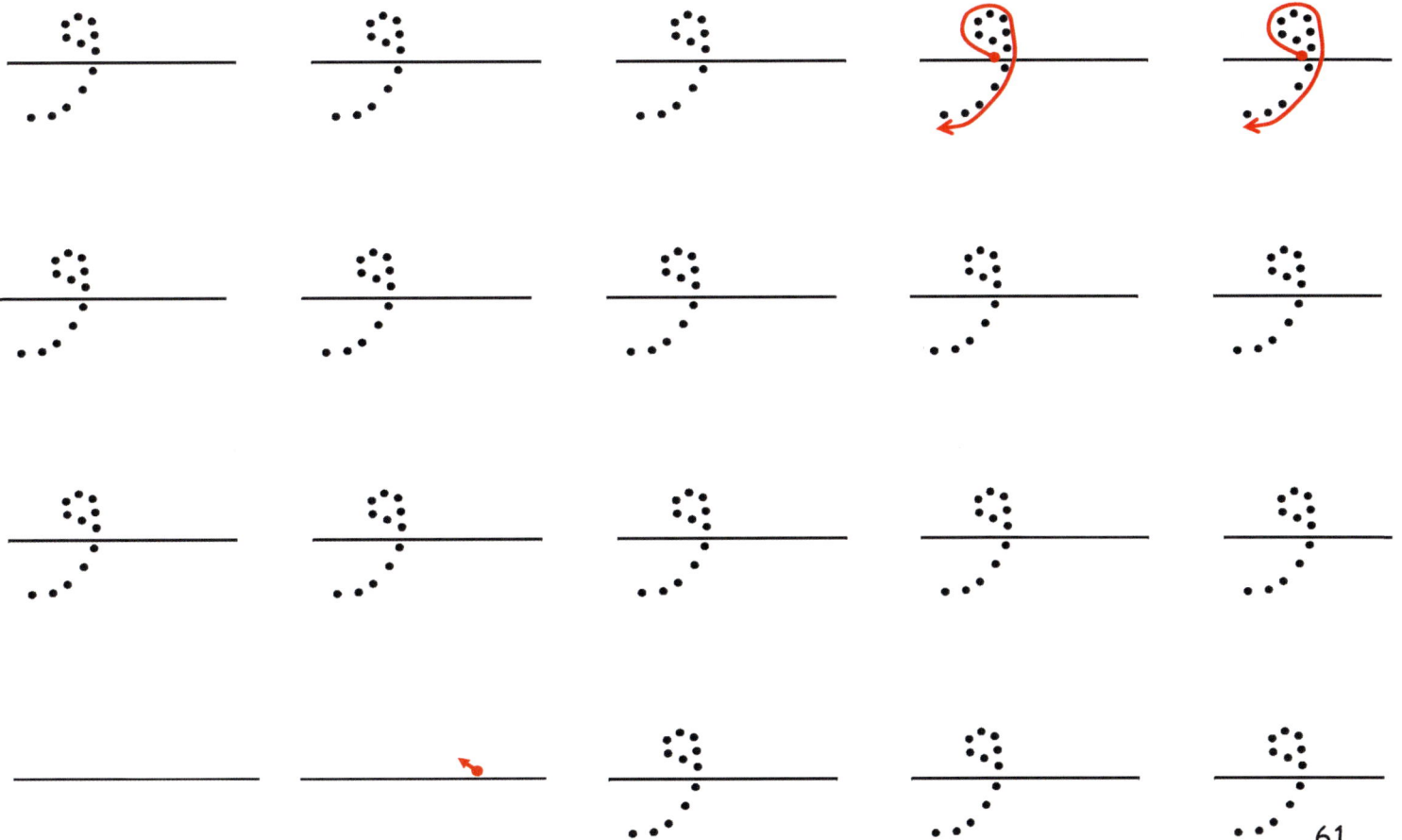

61

و

و

دَلْوٌ

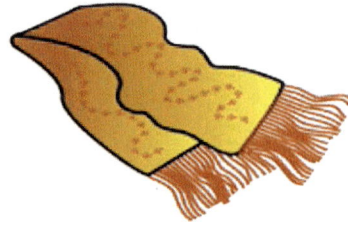

وِشَاحٌ

وو

و و و و و

ـو ـو ـو

او مو حو نو رو سو

سو طو عو فو فو كو

يو مو مو رو يو

Ya makes the sound 'ya' as in yard

يد Yad

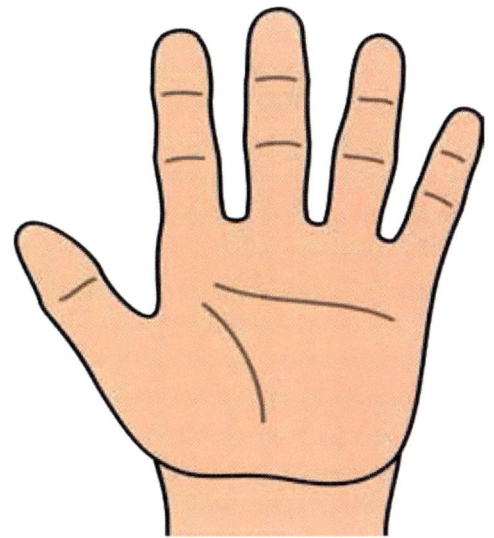

Read

ي ي ي ي ي ي

Write

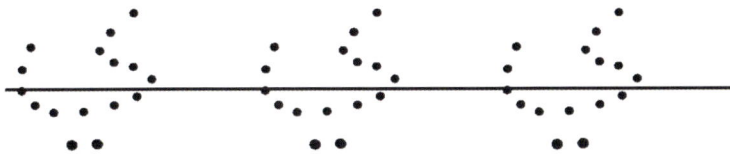 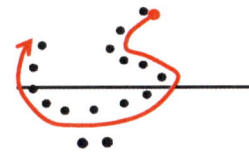 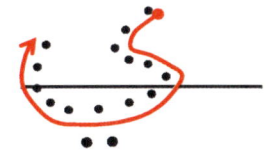

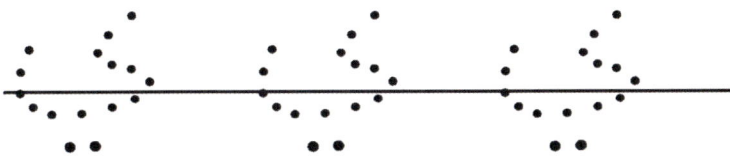 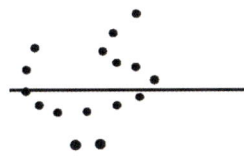 

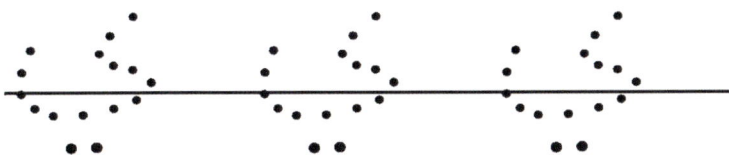 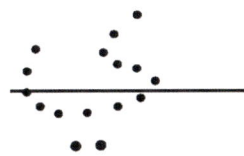 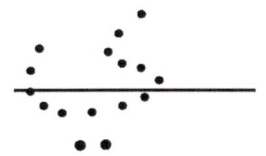

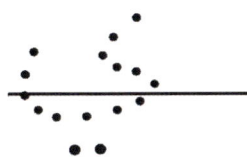 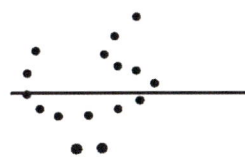 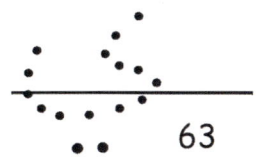

63

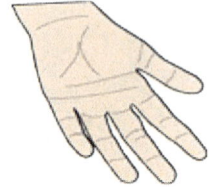

يَدٌ   لَيْمُونٌ   كُرْسِيٌّ

ي يـ ـيـ ـي

ـيـ ـيـ ـيـ ـيـ

ـيـ ـيـ ـيـ ـيـ ـيـ

ـي ـي ـي ـي

ـيـ ـيـ ـيـ

DID THIS BOOK HELP YOU OR OUR KID IN SOME WAY? IF SO, I'D LOVE TO HEAR ABOUT IT. HONEST REVIEWS HELP READERS FIND THE RIGHT BOOK FOR THEIR NEEDS.

FOR MORE PRACTICING ON ARABIC ALPHABETS YOU CAN SEARCH FOR:
"BIG ARABIC LETTERS TRACING WORKBOOK": FOR BIG SIZE LETTERS, EASY FOR BEGINNERS AND KIDS.
"ALIF BAA TAA ARABIC ALPHABET TRACING": FOR MORE PRACTICING ON ARABIC ALPHABETS.

Made in the USA
Las Vegas, NV
01 November 2021